T0082323

Lawfare

Also by Geoffrey Robertson

Lawfare

How Russians, the Rich and the Government Try to Prevent Free Speech and How to Stop Them

Geoffrey Robertson KC

TLS

TLS Books
An imprint of HarperCollins*Publishers*
1 London Bridge Street
London SE1 9GF

The-TLS.co.uk

HarperCollins*Publishers*
Macken House, 39/40 Mayor Street Upper
Dublin 1, D01 C9W8, Ireland

First published in Great Britain in 2023 by TLS Books

1

A catalogue record for this book is
available from the British Library

ISBN 978-0-00-860789-0

Typeset in Publico Text
Printed and bound in the UK using 100%
renewable electricity at CPI Group (UK) Ltd

To the memory of Paul Klebnikov, journalist
and client, sued for libel in London then
murdered in Moscow in revenge for
his work – or, possibly, for mine.

Contents

Lawfare

1.

The Weapons of Lawfare

The Ogre does what ogres can,
Deeds quite impossible for Man,
But one prize is beyond his reach,
The Ogre cannot master Speech.
About a subjugated plain,
Among its desperate and slain,
The Ogre stalks with hands on hips,
While drivel gushes from his lips.

'August 1968', W.H. Auden's depiction of Leonid Brezhnev's invasion of Czechoslovakia, applies with even greater force to Vladimir Putin as he gushes lies to justify his barbaric attack on Ukraine. These lies are, for people in Russia, 'facts' and his lickspittle MPs have rushed through a law to make it a crime for anyone to deny them by publishing the truth. Such censorship is anathema to a nation like Britain, which boasts of its history and tradition of 'free speech'. But wait a minute: as a top court once pointed out:

> Free speech does not mean free speech: it means
> speech hedged in by all the laws against
> defamation, blasphemy, sedition, and so forth. It
> means freedom governed by law.*

And, as this book will show, governed by lawyers, who act for the very rich to wage a bloodless but nonetheless scary war, in the form of litigation, against those who attempt to criticise or expose them. 'Lawfare' in this sense has come to mean the use of legal strategies to harass or intimidate publishers – to make them pay, literally, in large and unrecoverable (even if they win) legal fees, and in heavy damages and their own legal fees if they lose. This is not a new problem, but it has come into recent focus as publishers of prescient books about Putin have been frightened and deterred by lawyers acting for his oligarch friends, threatened with legal costs that can run to millions of pounds. You cannot blame lawyers for using the law. But that law is antipathetic to serious journalism and must be reformed if the Fourth Estate is to function effectively in our democracy by scrutinising the wealthy and the powerful.

* * *

---

* Privy Council, *James v. Commonwealth of Australia* (1936) AC 578.

'Lawfare' is a weak pun, with a pejorative tinge when used by those on the receiving end of writs for libel and breach of privacy. The term originated in America in the 1950s, when first used by army chiefs who objected to legal actions brought by civil liberties groups over discrimination in the military. In Australia, 'lawfare' has been denounced by government ministers upset by environmentalists whose lawyers have closed down coal mines, and in Brazil the label was hung on the right-wing judicial organs that concocted corruption allegations against the country's once and future president, Lula da Silva. Israel disparagingly accused pro-Palestinian activists of 'lawfare' when they tried to stop its foreign minister from coming to London, but its own supporters in the US, who fund legal actions against supporters of sanctions on Israel, call themselves 'the Lawfare Project'. In Britain, perhaps the best example of 'lawfare' against freedom of speech was Mrs Thatcher's courtroom crusade to stop newspapers from reporting any details of former MI5 officer Peter Wright's autobiography *Spycatcher*, while many copies of the book were being sold in the US and around the world. The word came into current vogue in Britain in 2022 as a description of the work of 'reputation lawyers' who had been issuing threats and writs against authors and publishers of books about Russian oligarchs, many of whom would be sanctioned by the British government after their friend and benefactor Vladimir Putin invaded Ukraine.

The most notable victim was a distinguished journalist, Catherine Belton, author of *Putin's People: How the KGB Took Back Russia and Then Took on the West*, which attracted a sudden blizzard of legal actions, from Roman Abramovich and three other oligarchs, and from Rosneft, Russia's national oil company, claiming that the book libelled them. It was estimated that this would cost her publishers £10 million to fight successfully, and more than twice as much if they lost – a real prospect because of the unfair rule in English libel cases that the defendant bears the burden of proof of truth and other defences. There had been preliminary skirmishes before the case settled, at a cost to HarperCollins of £1.5 million in legal fees and a cost to Belton of a year of stress and exhaustion in defending statements of great public interest that she believed were true. The court-enforced settlement was, as usual, strictly confidential, so the public cannot appreciate what infringements of free speech its terms require.

This is the perennial problem of defending allegations about Russians, and wealthy claimants from the Middle East, or indeed from Britain, namely the impossibility of proving truth when it is hidden behind offshore trusts or in tax havens or has come from sources who fear reprisals. The law of libel, unlike any other civil law, puts the

4

burden of proof on the defence, and however firmly and reasonably the author believes a defamatory statement, they must nevertheless prove its truth by evidence that is admissible in court. This is the main reason why, at a count some years ago, 95 per cent of libel claims were either won or settled on terms that required withdrawal of the allegations.

The Belton case became notorious, settled as it was some months before Putin went to war. The claimants certainly were not in need of money and *Putin's People* had been published a year before they took action: the flurry of writs came only after Alexei Navalny, Putin's political foe, had displayed the book at a public meeting. The legal actions were initially heard by a judge, who (as British judges usually do) found that the book bore a number of defamatory meanings, which means merely that it tends seriously to lower a claimant in the estimation of 'right thinking' people. The judge sent the case forward to a multi-million-pound trial. This was a political lesson for the UK media – defame Putin and his cronies at your peril.

They hardly needed it: over the previous few years, books had gone unwritten, or had been censored or simply not published, for fear of defamation actions about statements reasonably believed to be true but which were not capable of proof by evidence admissible in a British court. Typical was a book by

Karen Dawisha, *Putin's Kleptocracy: Who Owns Russia?*, which was turned down by Cambridge University Press. Its editor praised her manuscript, but wrote in rejection: 'The risk is high that those implicated in the premise of the book – that Putin has a close circle of criminal oligarchs at his disposal and has spent his career cultivating this circle – would be motivated to sue.'* The editor added that even if they won, the costs would be ruinous – another reason why the UK's claim to be a land of 'free' speech is asinine when it comes to investigation of things that really matter. Especially when those investigations cast apersions on people of great wealth.

Such people are embraced by British judges. As one judge recently said of an international businessman, 'his professional achievements and family wealth make him a rare member of a small elite in the world of business. Members of this elite class are attracted to London ... and it is in the public interest that the reputation of such people should not be unlawfully damaged. Their business activities are of importance to the economic wellbeing of this country.' An importance that all too often judges permit to outweigh freedom of critical speech about their business activities.

---

* 'How Putin's Oligarchs Bought London', *New Yorker*, 17 March 2022.

But it is the current state of British law that allows this. There could scarcely be more worthy news than the reporting of the Panama Papers – a trove of offshore financial records leaked from the law firm Mossack Fonseca in 2016 – and the Paradise Papers hacked from Bermudan law firm Appleby, demonstrating the tax-dodging behaviour of politicians, multinationals, oligarchs and even royalty. The Paradise Papers were published worldwide in 2017 by ninety-four news organisations, but only the British – the BBC and the *Guardian* – were sued, for breach of confidence. They settled with Appleby, on terms that were, as usual, kept secret – a secrecy that is unacceptable in free speech cases, where the public should have a right to know the conditions on which news organisations – public ones, in the case of the BBC – agree to surrender their right to free speech. It is now being sued by a wealthy businessman who has donated £800,000 to the Conservative Party and is likely to spend more than that on lawyers, money that will be recouped from the BBC if he wins.

The SLAPP

It took a threat of real war to wake members of Parliament up to lawfare. Their counter-offensive, however, was aimed at reputation lawyers, who were named, blamed and shamed for offering 'legal intimidation services to the corrupt, to organised crime, to the Russian state or to its proxies'. They were 'white collar collaborators' who had 'corrupted the British justice system'. It did not occur to these fulminating MPs that perhaps it was the British justice system that was unjust, being tilted against freedom of expression long before Putin's friends took advantage of it.

But this time action was promised 'quickly and effectively' by the minister of justice, namely an 'anti-SLAPP' law and a modern Bill of Rights with a presumption in favour of freedom of speech – nothing less, or so Dominic Raab claimed, than a 'free speech revolution'. How false this claim turned out to be, when his bill was published in June 2022, will be explained in Chapter 5.

SLAPP stands for 'strategic lawsuits against public participation' – a nonsense name dreamed up by American academics. In the US, thirty-four states have adopted anti-SLAPP laws, enabling judges to strike out defamation and privacy claims which abuse the legal process because their primary objective is to stop legitimate reporting. This is not a difficult task for an American judge, who can readily dismiss claims that undermine the First Amendment to the US Constitution, which protects speech unless it is not only mistaken but also made maliciously or recklessly. Anti-SLAPP action may be taken immediately after the abusive suit is filed, and (this is rare in the US) legal costs may be awarded to the media defendant.

It can also have what Americans call 'the Streisand effect', after an anti-SLAPP order ended the actress's lawsuit against an environmentalist group that photographed her edge-of-cliff mansion in Malibu – as part of a scientific study of coastal erosion. Although only four members of the public had downloaded the pictures before she took action, hundreds of thousands downloaded them afterwards. (In Britain this can be called 'the *Spycatcher* effect' – over a million copies of the book were eventually sold as a result of all the publicity.) Anti-SLAPP laws work in the US because there is a constitutional guarantee of free speech, but they cannot work in Britain at present because lawyers will easily persuade judges that their clients, like everyone else, are entitled to access to justice.

The reluctance of British judges to accept that SLAPP-type suits should be dismissed was exemplified by the recent libel case brought by billionaire Arron Banks, the self-styled 'bad boy' of Brexit, against investigative journalist Carole Cadwalladr, over a TED Talk she gave in Canada in 2019 which had accused him of unlawful acceptance of Russian money. The case caused her great distress and loss of time, eventually involving a three-day ordeal in the witness box, and she had only been able to defend it by raising money through crowdfunding. Her lawyers insisted that she had been a victim of a SLAPP, but the judge would have none of this: the allegation was serious and Banks was entitled to have his day – many of them – in court.

Cadwalladr's allegation, although reasonably believed by the journalist to be true at the time she made it, was in fact false, as was later established in an inquiry by the National Crime Agency. Cadwalladr had in consequence been forced to drop her pleading that it was true, and to rely on the defence that it was in the public interest, which eventually succeeded as the judge found that she had acted reasonably at the time she gave the talk, and it was plainly in the public interest to find out if Russian money was helping to finance the Brexit campaign (so much so that the National Crime Agency had undertaken its inquiry).

In any event, after his public exoneration, Banks could not claim that the defamation remained 'serious'. But once a defamatory allegation has been found to be seri-ous, judges will not prevent it going ahead for trial, no matter how wealthy and powerful the claimant and how much they might wish to silence a critic rather than to win more money. There should of course be a power for judges to stop any libel action when its continuation could serve no remedial purpose – a point reached when Banks was cleared by the NCA. Instead the case continued to take up the time of the court and the money of the crowdfunders, until it concluded with a four-hundred-paragraph judgment, which Mr Banks has now been given leave to appeal.*

Defamation and Privacy

Oppressive lawsuits did not begin with the arrival of the kleptocrats and their reputation lawyers – the firm of Sue, Grabbit and Runne has been in business for many years. Such actions began in the 1970s when the financier Sir James Goldsmith hit on a novel way of closing down *Private Eye* by suing not only the magazine but all its distributors and the newsagents who stocked it. The Court of Appeal said that all of Goldsmith's cases could go ahead, on the basis that it could not be an abuse of the

---

* The appeal was listed for hearing on 23 February 2023, when the Court of Appeal will consider the correctness of the judge's novel approach that Banks's pre-trial exoneration meant that the defamation no longer did serious harm. This approach is logical, but libel law has never been logical.

law to use it. Then came Robert Maxwell, who would fire off a volley of writs at anyone who dared to take his name in vain. After that came the multinational McDonald's, which brought a massive defamation action against two young and penniless activists for distributing fifty copies of an ill-printed leaflet, in order to silence their (to some extent justified) criticism of the fast food chain.

Libel law has remained tilted in favour of wealthy claimants because any defence must be proved by the defendant – not only truth, but the other defences of honest opinion and public interest. Parliament made a few adjustments in the Defamation Act of 2013, which at least required claimants to show 'serious harm' to their reputation, but otherwise failed to remedy the unfair burden of proof that is placed heavily upon the media defendant in libel cases. The Act even abolished the only thing that oligarchs and multinationals feared about suing in English courts, namely trial by jury, the 'gang of twelve', which, unlike a judge, might see them for what they are.

The only real reforms in this area have come from the European Court of Human Rights – it condemned the contempt of court law that stopped the *Sunday Times* from exposing the Thalidomide scandal, and it insisted on protection of journalists' sources. This principle, essential to investigative journalism, had never been acknowledged by English judges. It was the Eurocourt that finally freed *Spycatcher* and directed a cap on libel damages, which had reached £1.5 million. As a result of the cap (at present, £300,000), damages are dwarfed by legal costs that can be counted in millions and which the loser must pay.

This book focuses on defects in what is termed 'the common law' – that part of the law of England that is made and developed by judges, as distinct from statute law, passed by Parliament. English judges, with some exceptions, have no feel for, or even understanding of, freedom of speech, for all their encomiums to it. Judges, not Parliament, have fashioned the most recent threat to press freedom – the sprawling growth of a law against the invasion of privacy.

Britain (to its discredit) had no protection for privacy at all until the 1998 Human Rights Act reproduced Article 8 of the European Convention on Human Rights: 'Everyone has the right to respect for his private and family life, his home and his correspondence.' 'Respect' is fine, unless the public interest requires exposure of mansions bought with laundered money or the use of family trusts to avoid tax, or a 'private' life that is abusive of a partner, or confidential documents that show corruption. The public interest may justify publication, but wealthy complainants can readily put a stop to this by obtaining an injunction, forbidding release of any information in relation to which they claim a 'reasonable expectation of privacy'. They simply sue for the civil wrong (called a tort) of 'misuse of private information' and obtain injunctions readily enough by showing that they are more likely than not to succeed at trial. The information – no matter how important – cannot be published and media defendants often give up at this point because news is a perishable commodity and a trial could take years, or because of the prohibitive costs of an eventual trial, whether they win or lose.

Article 8 of the European Convention was drawn up under the shadow of the trials of Nazi leaders at Nuremberg, and was intended to stop states from ever again permitting a Gestapo, without warrant, to make that 'early morning knock on the door'. So how has it been extended to the point today where it allows dodgy businessmen and their companies to stop the media from revealing truthful facts about their operations or wealthy men to gag their ex-wives from speaking out about an abusive relationship?

The rot began, fairly precisely, in 2004–5, when both the top court in the UK (then the House of Lords Judicial Committee) and the European Court of Human Rights decided that two rather precious and much-photographed women, respectively the supermodel Naomi Campbell* and Princess Caroline von Hannover of

---

* *Campbell v. MGN Ltd* (2004) 2AC 457.

Monaco,* had a reasonable expectation of privacy when they walked down a public street. These highly questionable results were reached by majority decision. Ms Campbell had strongly denied that she had ever used illegal drugs, but she was photographed entering Narcotics Anonymous. Princess Caroline was a fashionable celebrity who was part of Monaco's royal family and sometimes took on official duties, but the Eurocourt ruled that she must be protected from publication of harmless photographs showing her shopping and horse-riding. Her right to privacy 'extended beyond the family circle and included a social dimension or a zone of interaction even in a public context'.

For this incoherent reason, an enforceable right of privacy over social and financial networks was soon being claimed by kleptocrats and conmen alike, upheld on these two precedents by sympathetic judges, unless the defendant could prove corruption. In 2019 the NGO Global Witness managed to do so when it acquired bank statements of the son of the president of the Congo, which showed his corrupt use of credit cards, paid from state funds, to buy hundreds of thousands of pounds' worth of luxury goods. But his reputation lawyers had no difficulty in taking the case, and even managed to obtain a short-term injunction, against a cash-strapped NGO

---

* *Princess Caroline v. Germany* (2005) 40 EHRR1.

reliant on pro-bono legal help. Privacy law, it must be remembered, serves to suppress information that is true.

So privacy actions proliferate, to deter or freeze investigative journalism, by suppressing information that is factual. The courts consider that 'a reasonable expectation of privacy' covers a very wide field, not only one's physical or mental health, but 'racial or ethnic characteristics ... the generality of personal and family relationships; ... information conveyed in the course of personal relationships; a person's political opinions and affiliations; a person's religious commitment; personal financial and tax related information; personal communications and correspondence; matters pertaining to the home; past involvement in criminal behaviour; involvement in civil litigation concerning private affairs; and involvement in crime as a victim or a witness'.*

Any self-respecting kleptocrat with a mansion and a superyacht and a tax-avoidance scheme has a vast amount of information he or she can call on the courts to protect from exposure, unless the defending author or journalist can prove (the burden of proof, of course, being on the defendant) that publication serves an overriding public interest. And the public interest in freedom of speech is not enough: most cases will involve information that has been obtained from companies or

---

* *Bloomberg LP v. ZXC* (2022) UKSC 5, para 52, 2022 2 WLR 424.

government departments in breach of confidence, so judges say that keeping confidences is in the public interest as much as, or even more than, freedom of speech. So the law does not pit one person's privacy against everyone's right of free speech – it favours privacy unless it can be outweighed in what is called a 'balancing exercise' with the public interest. But this judicial balancing exercise is a nonsense – the two cannot sensibly be compared. All it means is that judges impose their own prejudices and preferences to decide which is to prevail. Most High Court judges spend their professional lives as commercial lawyers, and have a property-based outlook when it comes to balancing a right to keep commercial secrets against the right of free speech: for them, this is like balancing hard cash against hot air.

And so the claimant usually wins, the public interest notwithstanding. As did Cliff Richard, after a police team was granted a search warrant by a compliant magistrate to search his mansion in 2014. The pop star obtained heavy damages – and rightfully so – against the negligent police force that had acted without credible evidence, but went on to obtain hundreds of thousands in damages, and reportedly millions in costs, against the BBC.* The corporation may have been over-enthusiastic in hiring a helicopter to cover the raid, but the newsworthiness of

---

* *Richard v. BBC* (2018) EWHC 1837.

the execution of a search warrant which should never have been granted on the home of a public figure could hardly be doubted – other than by a judge. Sir Cliff was soon vindicated – his name had been besmirched, but by the police acting without reasonable evidence, not by the BBC which had reported on an abuse of police power.

In order to award him damages, the High Court decided that all suspects had a 'reasonable expectation of privacy' at any stage of a police investigation, no matter how long it was taking or how important the suspect. That meant a severe handicap to the 'watchdog' function of the media in respect of the police, because journalists could not fully report on their dealings with suspects if they could not report their names or what they were suspected of having done wrong.

But this ruling was applied by the UK's Supreme Court in 2022 to prevent Bloomberg from reporting a highly significant development in tackling corruption.* The public judgment is littered with unnecessary name redactions, but it appears that a journalist from Bloomberg News got hold of an official request, presumably by the Serious Fraud Office, and apparently to the courts of Hong Kong, to provide information about an allegedly crooked businessman and his company, frequently named and criticised in the UK Parliament.

---

* *Bloomberg LP v. ZXC*, op. cit.

These allegations had often been reported in the media, and what was newsworthy was the fact that a law-enforcement agency was finally doing something about them. The request to the Hong Kong courts for information about a suspected corporation and its official – both widely alleged to have been engaged in corruption – was of obvious public interest, and it would have served as a basis for follow-up enquiries as to whether the Hong Kong courts had complied, or whether (if, say, the claimant or the company had connections with the Chinese government) they had refused.

But the Supreme Court merely ruled that Mr ZXC had a 'reasonable expectation' that investigations into his alleged corruption should be kept private. As a Supreme Court decision, the Bloomberg case carries great weight. A month or so after it was delivered, it deterred the Metropolitan Police, and then the press, from revealing the names of persons who had been issued with fines for attending Downing Street parties in breach of Covid rules, unless they chose to 'out' themselves. At the time of writing, in 2022, it was preventing publication of the name of a Conservative MP arrested for rape.

What is striking is that none of the Supreme Court judges could discern any public interest in publishing the names of suspects, even though it is well known (especially in rape cases) that doing this often causes more witnesses to come forward – sometimes with evidence of other crimes, and occasionally with evidence that exonerates the suspect. It is also a boon to the watchdog function of the press to alert the public to the behaviour of law enforcers, which is often ineffective or incompetent or over-zealous (see the disgraceful behaviour of the Met in Operation Midland, searching without good reason the homes of Lords Brittan and Bramall, and former MP Harvey Proctor). The Supreme Court members seemed oblivious to these public goods, which were incapable of counterbalancing the privacy right claimed by Mr ZXC and his company, X Ltd. The full story – including their real names – was set out in the court's 'closed' judgment.

This is a phenomenon now found frequently in privacy cases. Judges set out their legal reasoning in an 'open' judgment, with their full analysis of the facts in a separate judgment, which they 'close'. This is not a procedure authorised by Parliament, and it runs counter to the 'open justice' principle of English law – the requirement for justice to be seen to be done. But like privacy claims, it has grown like Topsy, and nobody quite knows where these closed judgments go or who may gain access to them or when. Academics seem incurious and the Ministry of Justice itself, which presumably provides storage space somewhere, is unforthcoming. Are they ever catalogued or indexed, can they be destroyed, will they be published only after the death of the claimant, can judges look at them again if they realise they were misled? So many legitimate questions, but no clear answers, which is a common problem with judge-made law on confusing and controversial subjects like the right to privacy. And, of course, it prevents criticism of the judges by experts who might otherwise conclude that their judgments were mistaken.

But if judges are not much good these days as protectors of free speech, Parliament is even worse. In 2018 it passed another flail for the media's back, a new Data Protection Act, which made it a crime (with potentially large fines) to publish any 'data' about a person that had not been approved by a 'data controller'. This provides a means of punishing journalists' sources, namely whistleblowers, who provide them with information which usually includes personal data, and is usually in breach of the whistleblower's employment contract. The UK's information commissioner has wide enforcement powers: in 2021 she decided to raid the homes of persons suspected of leaking to the media CCTV stills of Health Secretary Matt Hancock in his office embracing his girlfriend, in breach of his own Covid guidelines. It took public ridicule to force the commissioner to back down, but in theory the source for that sensational photograph could have been found guilty of a crime for making it available to newspapers. There is a weak public interest defence, but Parliament of course has placed its proof on the defendant.

Oligarchs now have two grounds for stopping, or suing over, revelation of the truth about their personal or business affairs. They can demand injunctions and damages for the common-law newly beefed-up tort of 'misuse of private information', and (additionally, not alternatively) they can obtain injunctions and compensation for damage or 'distress' over breaches of the Data Protection Act. 'Personal data' has the widest of meanings and covers virtually any truth obtained about a claimant, however important for the public to know, if acquired by a source in breach of duties owed to their employer. Most media 'scoops' come about in this way, including the revelations several years ago about how politicians were making outlandish expenses claims – to build their duck houses, for example – and these cumulative privacy laws add further terrors to investigative journalism. They have public interest defences, of course, but these are vague and the burden of proving them falls, at great expense, on the publisher.

The Legal Marketplace

Journalism is a career but not a profession. It is the exercise by occupation of the right to freedom of expression available to every citizen. It cannot in principle be withdrawn from a few by government licensing or professional registration, but it can be restricted by rules of law.

For journalists, 'free speech' is, in practice, what remains of speech after lawyers have had their say. The array of media laws is formidable – not only defamation and privacy and data protection, but official secrets and contempt of court and copyright – and publishing companies and broadcasters employ teams of lawyers (once called 'night lawyers', but they now work 24/7) to censor and sanitise stories that might court reprisals. These media lawyers can be more repressive than media laws because their advice will generally err on the safe side, where they cannot be proved wrong. 'If in doubt, cut it out' was the motto pinned to the wall of the first media lawyer for whom I worked as an articled clerk. The lawyers' advice provides a broad penumbra of restraint, confining journalists not to the letter of the law but to an outer rim bounded by the mere possibility of legal action. Journalists must be on the defensive, asking themselves not 'What should I write?' but 'What can I write that will get past the lawyers?' – whose caution is understandable when they are employed or instructed by proprietors who want to avoid the massive legal costs of defending, even successfully, actions brought by embarrassed governments or by irate billionaires.

The reason why lawyers tend to be overcautious in advising publishers is that they can be sued for negligence if they 'clear' a story which subsequently leads to a prosecution or a civil action against their client. I was caught out once, when I told the *New Statesman* it could publish an interview with a member of the jury that had acquitted Jeremy Thorpe. They had all thought Thorpe was guilty of murder, but had been told by the judge not to convict on the evidence of the main prosecution witness, former Liberal MP Peter Bessell, because he had accepted a deal offered by the *Daily Telegraph*: £25,000 down, and a further £25,000 if his evidence secured Thorpe's conviction. This was outrageous, and important for the public to know, but the *Guardian* (whose journalist had conducted the interview) was afraid to publish it.

I advised the *New Statesman*'s editor, Bruce Page, that there was no law to stop him, but the attorney general disagreed and prosecuted him, although he should have prosecuted the editor of the *Telegraph*, whose deal with Bessell amounted to a perversion of justice. I assumed that the *New Statesman* would retain an eminent QC to defend them (I had only been a barrister for a couple of years) but Bruce had other ideas: 'You advised us to publish, so you must be the best person to defend your advice.' (I was also the cheapest.) I did so successfully,* but the legal establishment was appalled at the prospect

---

* *Attorney General v. New Statesman* [1981] Queen's Bench p. 1.

of free speech for jurors – so the government rushed a new law through Parliament with two years' imprisonment for revealing or publishing 'secrets of the jury room', no matter how important to expose a miscarriage of justice or how insightful about jury behaviour – as, in the past, articles written by Graham Greene, Alan Coren and others had certainly been. Although I have said that the UK is a land of expensive rather than free speech, in relation to cases brought under the Official Secrets Act, or about jury revelations, it is a land which allows no speech at all. There is no public interest defence in either case.

Sometimes journalists feel that their published story looks like the tip of an iceberg – the information they wanted to publish lies below, deep frozen by their lawyers' caution. Especially after receiving the usual bumptious and bullying letters so favoured by the coterie of reputation lawyers anxious to earn their exorbitant fees by commencing the interminable round of pre-trial hearings, once described by the Court of Appeal as an 'archaic saraband' (a stately Spanish dance in triple time). Costs are driven up by court protocols (requiring polite but detailed replies to the demands of the claimant's lawyers) and pre-trial hearings to decide issues about the meaning of the words, disclosure of each side's documents, and the like. Gone are the days of *Arkell v. Pressdram*, when a famous reputation lawyer (Lord Goodman) ended his letter before action:

> Mr Arkell's first concern is that there should be a
> full retraction at the earliest possible date in
> Private Eye and he will also want his costs paid.
> His attitude to damages will be governed by the
> nature of your reply.

To which the magazine responded:

> We note that Mr Arkell's attitude to damages will
> be governed by the nature of our reply and would
> therefore be grateful if you could inform us what
> his attitude to damages would be, were he to learn
> that the nature of our reply is as follows: fuck off.

Mr Arkell and his celebrity lawyer did so, their bluff called. But robust responses of this kind are now prohibited by an official 'pre-action protocol' and the opposing solicitors are politely partnered for the saraband. The pre-action protocol was introduced by Lord Chancellor Derry Irvine with good intentions, but it has proved a gift for lawfare lawyers because it puts the publisher on the back foot immediately. The claimant must open by giving a 'sufficient explanation' as to why the defendant's conduct is 'insupportable'. This often produces a multitude of bullying letters, frothing with righteous indignation on behalf of clients, exaggerating the meaning of offending words and ending with a threat to win heavy damages unless the defendant apologises by way of a statement in open court, pays some damages and all the claimant's costs thus far.

The protocol goes on, onerously, to require a response from the defendant explaining the reasons for rejecting the claim and demanding details of any facts on which the defendant proposes to rely. An *Arkell v. Pressdram* response is no longer possible, and the protocol puts the media defendant on the defensive from the outset, given so little time to marshal all the facts that may be necessary to prove truth.

Exchanges of letters often go on for more than a year with hearings in court to decide meanings, which the journalist must defend, and to referee disputes over disclosure of documents (claimants will be particularly keen to discover the journalists' sources, in order to threaten them with legal action as well). KCs will be hired at up to £900 an hour to advise and deal with court hearings, and it does not take long for a million pounds to be racked up in fees before the trial has even started. Journalists complained to a parliamentary enquiry on SLAPPs that in this period they were sometimes subjected to surveillance and harassment by private eyes, ex-police or ex-MI5 'security consultants', ex-GCHQ operatives and other spies hired by the wealthy claimant or his solicitor or his public relations company. It is a lengthy and expensive game of bluff and counter-bluff, and often the publisher will 'pay to make it go away' by settling and removing the words, however true, that have been made the subject of complaint.

Unlike America, where lawyers divide into a 'plaintiffs bar' and those dedicated to defending the media, the London defamation industry is made up of a handful of solicitor firms and a dozen or so 'top KCs' with twice as many juniors, specialising in media law and in acting both for claimants and defendants. Big publishers will have in-house lawyers, but cases that come to court will involve solicitors and counsel who specialise in a subject with centuries of precedents and textbooks of a thousand or so pages elucidating arcane principles like 'the repetition rule', under which a journalist can be sued for relying on a defamatory statement made by someone else, no matter how often it has been previously published or how significant the source. (This rule, which enriched Princess Elizabeth of Toro, see p. 54, and Jani Allan, see p. 82, is a particular plague on public interest reportage.) Occasionally, if an appellant can afford to risk a million pounds or so, a media case may reach the Supreme Court, where it is a matter of luck whether judges with brilliant legal minds but no background in the subject will understand free speech and develop the law to encourage it, or show no interest at all and deliver judgments that could impede it further. In 2003, the *Wall Street Journal* was fortunate to strike judges like Brenda Hale, Tom Bingham and Leonard Hoffmann who believed in investigative journalism and fashioned a public interest defence for it, but in 2022 Bloomberg was not so lucky with the current Supreme Court whose members did not seem to recognise its importance and fashioned privacy law which will work to discourage it.

Defendants often throw in the towel simply because they cannot afford the escalating pre-trial costs, let alone those of the trial itself. Surrender is usually signalled by a 'statement in open court' – a form of ritual humiliation in which the claimant's lawyers proclaim their client's good character and innocence of the published allegations, and the defendant's lawyer stands up to bend the knee and mutter agreement. Judges are anxious to encourage settlements and do not look at these statements very closely – they are the deal by which the defendant media saves further costs. Often the statement will boast that the claimant's reputation has been vindicated by payment of 'significant' or 'substantial' damages, although the public are never told the amount (in some cases, it is neither).

Why is it important to change the law in favour of investigative journalism? Perhaps the greatest scandal of the present century so far was how Jimmy Savile was allowed to go on his paedophile rampage through children's homes and BBC studios. Was this the fault of a lazy media, incapable of performing the watchdog role of the press? No, it was the fault of the burden of proof in libel cases. As early as 1994, the *Sunday Mirror* had collected enough evidence to suspect that the entertainer had abused children, but the paper's QC said that it failed the 'burden of proof' test: it did not prove Savile's misconduct to a high enough standard, and would incur a massive sum in costs and damages when he sued them over such an outrageous libel. In 2008 the *Sun* obtained signed statements from several of Savile's victims at an orphanage in Jersey – but would these vulnerable women stand up to cross-examination on behalf of a man whose character witnesses would include Baroness Thatcher and Prince Charles? The *Sun*'s QC said they could probably not shoulder the burden of proof, so the paper decided not to risk millions (and perhaps the hostility of its readers) by publishing. The *Sun* did have an 'exclusive' picture of the paedophile with some girls in care at the home, which it published with a caption it knew to be a lie: 'Sir Jimmy had no idea of the horrors at the orphanage.' It may well have said otherwise, had the burden of proof been on the claimant, as it is in every other civil action.*

---

* See Merion Jones, 'Outrageous Libel Laws Protected Jimmy Savile', *Guardian*, 28 April 2022.

2.

Why Free Speech?

Think of what our Nation stands for,
Books from Boots' and country lanes,
Free speech, free passes, class distinction,
Democracy and proper drains.*

In Betjeman's England, 'free speech' washes like fluoride through the suburban water supply, but as a cultural assumption rather than as a constitutional right. When liberty exists as a state of mind, unprotected by legal rights, it gets limited when uncongenial to people with real power, assisted by those George Orwell termed 'the striped-trousered ones who rule' – notably judges, Treasury solicitors and reputation lawyers. As Orwell pointed out in the introduction to *Animal Farm* (which his left-wing publisher turned down because it insulted Stalin), 'If liberty means anything at all, it means the right to tell people what they do not want to hear' – an

---

* John Betjeman, 'In Westminster Abbey'.

aphorism engraved on his statue outside the BBC as a spur to the corporation to resist government pressure. But investigative journalism remains a struggle to tell inconvenient truths, against the wishes not merely of governments, but of oligarchs and wealthy public figures and powerful transnational corporations wishing to furbish their reputations.

Nonetheless, free speech lives not in our law but in our rhetoric and our national pride. It was described by justice secretary Dominic Raab as a 'quintessentially UK right ... a unique and precious liberty on which the UK has historically placed great emphasis in our traditions'.* This is nonsense. Magna Carta was silent on the subject in 1215, and in 1275 came our first statutory prohibition: the crime of *scandalum magnatum* to protect 'the great men of the realm' from speech that might arouse the public against them. Hence Lord Coke's maxim that 'the greater the truth, the greater the libel'. (He was explaining, with homely seventeenth-century sexism, that 'a woman would not grieve to be told she had a red nose, unless she had one'.) Criminal libel sent to jail those who discomfited great men of the realm, or the king or government. During the Civil War, Parliament decided to set up a board of 'the good and the wise' to license news-

---

* Human Rights Act Reform: A Modern Bill of Rights, Consultation Response, Ministry of Justice, 12 July 2022, p. 6.

papers, which led the poet John Milton to issue an immortal cry for press freedom, the *Areopagitica*, declaring that:

> Promiscuous reading is necessary to the constituting of human nature. The attempt to keep out evil doctrine by licensing is like the exploit of that gallant man who thought to keep out the crows by shutting his park gate.

However, during the Restoration a sinister figure emerged – a 'surveyor of the press', who spied out sedition and sent publishers to the gallows. Milton himself was lucky to escape, and his epic poem *Paradise Lost* was burned by the public hangman for suggesting that an eclipse of the sun 'with sudden fear of change perplexes monarchs'. It was forbidden to describe the king as perplexed, and in this period republican supporters were hunted down and strung up. Previously, in England's brief republic (the Interregnum of 1649 to 1660), the Levellers (who were not early socialists, but rather highly opinionated investigative journalists) saw their leader twice put on trial for treason. But John Lilburne found the Achilles heel in Oliver Cromwell's body politic – the jury, which both times stood up to the government and acquitted Lilburne for his incendiary pamphlets.

So did the jury that in 1670 acquitted the Quakers William Penn and William Mead for preaching their religion, despite the judge's direction to convict. Although locked up for two days without food or fire or even a chamber pot, the jurors insisted on returning a verdict of 'not guilty'. The government had them imprisoned for disobeying the judge, but ultimately the courts decided that jurors were entitled to follow their own consciences.

The juries that acquitted Lilburne and Penn held a candle for free speech that occasionally flickered in defamation trials in later centuries, until they were abolished in such cases by Nick Clegg and the Coalition Government in 2013.

William Caxton's printing press had begun rolling at Westminster in 1476, and it was not long before the king's judges in the Star Chamber devised ferocious punishments for sedition: by cutting off the ears of puritan preachers. A second offence meant the stumps of their ears would be cut off as well, with the letters 'SL' (for 'seditious libeller') burned into their foreheads. At the time of these barbaric penalties for political speech, the Star Chamber (in effect, the king's private court) was faced with the problem that too many great people in the realm were killing themselves in the course of settling their quarrels by duelling. So it devised an alternative to fighting a duel with pistols – a law of civil libel, which the judges soon developed in a way that was designed to encourage plaintiffs to hazard their money rather than their life, by a legal presumption that all defamatory statements were false. This presumption survives today although it is absurd (defamatory statements are often true, or at least partly true), and it remains the ludicrous reason why the burden of proof is thrown on the defendant.

Civil defamation became very fashionable in the nineteenth century, when political lives were lived in gentlemen's clubs, when escutcheons could be unblotted and society scandals resolved by writs for slander. It was an upper-class pursuit, and the main cases concerned allegations of cheating at cards or shooting foxes (highly defamatory, old chap: a real gentleman hunts down foxes with dogs). Usually the plaintiff won unless, like Oscar Wilde, he had a really bad QC.

The only free speech hero to emerge in later British history was John Wilkes, an MP and radical pamphleteer, who became a target of government for his newspaper, the *North Briton*, which excoriated George III. Wilkes's mistake was to publish in 1763 a parody of Alexander Pope – 'Essay on Woman' – which Lord Sandwich (he of the request for 'some meat between two slices of bread') decided was obscene and so read it to the House of Lords:

> Life can little more supply
> Than just a few good fucks
> And then we die.

He stopped, at this first utterance in Parliament of a four-letter word, but fellow peers shouted, 'Go on, go on.' Wilkes was jailed for obscene libel and disqualified, but re-elected – three times – while in prison. His great achievement was to outwit the home secretary, Lord Halifax, and the sinister blind Treasury solicitor who ordered raids on his home and office and printing press, and took a malicious pleasure in seizing his stock of condoms. Wilkes sued for, and received, large damages when the general warrants used by the government were declared illegal in a landmark ruling by the chief justice, Richard Pratt, on the basis that an Englishman's home was his castle.*

It was at this point, historians claim, that the London mob began the chant 'Wilkes and freedom of the press', although they underestimate mob intelligence – the actual chant was 'Wilkes, Pratt and freedom of the press'. Every hero journalist needs a good lawyer, and it would be two centuries before another judge, Lord Denning, would be celebrated, at least by himself, for taking this role.

---

* *Entick v. Carrington*, 19 State J 1029.

Nonetheless, and despite Charles James Fox's Libel Act of 1792, which made juries rather than judges the decision-makers in criminal libel trials, the government soon found ways to bribe juries to convict. Tom Paine, the former customs officer from Lewes, was its prime target. His pamphlet *Common Sense* notoriously inflamed the American revolution (Barack Obama read from it at his inauguration), and from his room at the Angel Tavern in Islington came those ringing demands for free speech and other liberties – *The Rights of Man* and later *The Age of Reason*. Any bookseller who stocked them was prosecuted and thrown into prison, with hard labour – some of the saddest passages in the old law reports record their pleas, never heeded by cruel judges, to spare their wives and children from destitution.

This was the great British tradition of free speech, at the time in America when James Madison and Alexander Hamilton were drafting the First Amendment. Only once in British history did members of Parliament ever think to enshrine free speech in our make-believe constitution, and that was to give themselves an absolute privilege against being sued for anything they said in Parliament.

This had been part of the 1689 Bill of Rights, which established the immunity of politicians from legal consequences for anything they said in either House. It stood unchanged for three hundred years, until one junior minister, Neil Hamilton MP, sued the *Guardian* newspaper for libel, for alleging that he had been paid by Mohamed al-Fayed 'cash for questions' he had asked in al-Fayed's interest, in the House of Commons. To Hamilton's horror, a judge ruled that his case could not go ahead because the Bill of Rights prevented courts from entertaining a legal action about motives behind anything said in the House.

So Hamilton prevailed on John Major and his complaisant Tory MPs to rush through an amendment that would permit them to sue anyone who criticised their conduct in Parliament, so long as they waived their own parliamentary privilege. Hamilton's libel action restarted, claiming heavy damages against a newspaper that had published nothing but the truth. Yet it is sadly typical of the British attitude to free speech that the one law which bestowed it, and only on members of Parliament, was amended to allow them to sue the media for large amounts of money for exposing their sleaziness. (Years later, after this case had exposed Hamilton as a liar, the amendment was repealed.)

The Bill of Rights immunity for MPs has occasionally been used, to the displeasure of the Speaker, for example to name Kim Philby as a spy (his spying had been hidden behind the Official Secrets Act), and by Lord Peter Hain to expose the fact that Sir Philip Green had been granted a super-injunction to stop the media reporting allegations about his sexist and racist behaviour. This free speech right had its greatest moment in 1979, during an official secrets trial of two journalists from *Time Out* charged with revealing the existence of GCHQ (the spy agency's activities were no secret to the Americans or the Russians, but were being kept from the British public by the Official Secrets Act). The prosecution expert on secrecy, called 'Colonel B' because his name and his job were said to be very secret, blew his own cover in answer to my questions, talking about his appearance in regimental magazines, which he helpfully identified, allowing journalists from *Peace News* to discover and publish his well-known name.

The attorney general prosecuted the paper – to the chagrin of the National Union of Journalists, holding its annual conference at a beachside resort. Its members wrote Colonel B's real name in large letters on the sand, to the fury of Special Branch, who set out from Scotland Yard to arrest them, but by the time the detectives arrived, the tide had washed away the evidence.

The next day in Parliament, while the Speaker was dozing after a heavy lunch, an obscure backbench MP, one Robert Kilroy-Silk (later much seen on television), slipped the dreaded name into a question, and was followed by three other Labour MPs. The attorney general and his director of public prosecutions telegraphed every broadcaster and national newspaper threatening to prosecute if they dared to report or publish the name. In a rare show of unanimity, the media declared that this was a constitutional outrage – the reporting of anything said in Parliament was protected by the Bill of Rights – and the name (Colonel H. A. Johnstone) featured in every news bulletin. It was the one time when the British media went on the offensive, because it had a right to do so and not merely a defence if it did.

The First Amendment came as a revulsion against the English common law of seditious libel. As Madison explained, the revolutionary US Constitution meant 'the people, not the government, possess the absolute sovereignty' and the people's newspapers could not be censored or suppressed by government or, in time, by anyone else. Not even, as the US Supreme Court ruled much later in the *Pentagon Papers* case, by a government on the grounds of national security:

> Any system of prior restraints of expression
> comes to this Court bearing a heavy presumption
> against its constitutional validity ... The only
> effective restraint upon executive policy and
> power in the areas of national defense and
> international affairs may lie in an enlightened
> citizenry – in an informed and critical public
> opinion which alone can here protect the values

of democratic government ... For without an
informed and free press there cannot be an
enlightened people.*

You don't get judgments like that in Britain, where judges bend over backwards to ban the likes of *Spycatcher* whenever they hear a claim, however exaggerated, of 'national security'.

As for defamation, litigants who would certainly succeed in the UK fail in the US, like the police chief who sued a newspaper for accusing him of mistreating demonstrators and ended up with his name adorning the famous 1964 ruling in *New York Times v. Sullivan*.† Applying the First Amendment to libel actions, the US Supreme Court ruled that no case brought by a public figure would be allowed to proceed against a publisher whose allegations were honestly and diligently made. (In 2022, Johnny Depp – a public figure – would have to establish that his ex-wife Amber Heard's allegations against him were malicious before he could recover

---

* *New York Times v. US* (1991) 403 US 713 at 729. The *Pentagon Papers* was a secret history of US involvement in the Vietnam War, leaked to the press by celebrated whistleblower Daniel Ellsberg, currently much occupied in supporting Julian Assange for doing much the same thing. English courts have thus far held that Assange cannot escape extradition to the US by virtue of the public interest in his revelations.

† 401 US 265 (1964).

damages.) The *New York Times* ruling freed the US media to probe Watergate and Enron and the bankers of 'Londonistan' and sex abuse scandals in the Catholic Church in a depth and detail that could never be attempted in Britain.

That this was so, well before the oligarchs descended on London, is exemplified by the success of one wealthy serial litigant, Robert Maxwell, who sued obsessively to protect his reputation and his business secrets, while raiding his employees' pensions. Only six months before his corporate dishonesty came to light after his death by drowning (probably after losing his balance when urinating off the deck of his superyacht), Maxwell had obtained an injunction from an obliging High Court judge which had banned the press from reporting the truth that he had 'engaged in dubious accounting devices' or had 'sought to mislead ... as to the values of the assets of his company'. This was a super-injunction, meaning the media were not even allowed to report that it had been obtained.

The villain had already secured the suppression of two books about his life and alleged crimes by threatening to sue not only their publishers, but any bookseller who dared to display them. He had persecuted one author, Tom Bower, personally, even by arranging for bailiffs to turn up at his home to foreclose on an imaginary debt. Maxwell did publish a grovelling hagiography of himself, written by his own employee. The suppression of the truth about him, long before the oligarchs came to London ('A town named Sue', as American journalists describe it), was just one example of how defamation law was already being used to deter investigative journalism.

That was the main reason why there was so very little of it, even in the twentieth century, at least until the 1960s when the *Sunday Times* under Harry Evans started its Insight Team reporting and began to fight back against legal attempts to suppress its investigations into Thalidomide and crooked international financiers. Throughout the 1930s the British press had been muzzled – or muzzled itself – and kept the public in the dark in the build-up to the scandal of the century: the abdication of Edward VIII. This was a matter on which the public should certainly have had a say, namely whether their king should be de-throned for marrying an American divorcee. Official secrecy was suffocating – the people were not allowed to know about the Suez Crisis until it was too late. In the 1960s the unfolding scandal over John Profumo was gagged by defamation – he gained time by winning damages against several newspapers for daring to suggest that he had slept with Christine Keeler.

So, contrary to the boasts of politicians such as Mr Raab, the United Kingdom has a wretched history and tradition when it comes to free speech. That is because of laws and procedures that for the most part remain in force.

The only boast that Britain can make is that it has no system for government licensing of the media – the censorship system railed against by Milton collapsed through corruption in 1697. But it has judges who can usually be relied on to do the government's bidding when 'national security' is put in play, as when the Thatcher government wanted to stop publication of *Spycatcher* because it was written by Peter Wright, the former MI5 officer who believed his director-general was a Russian agent. The government heard that the book was in the hands of my client, William Heinemann and Co., a respected publisher owned by the wealthy philanthropist Paul Hamlyn. In typically British fashion, the first step proved to be a call to his CEO from the Treasury Solicitor, who warned of crippling legal costs if the book went ahead – 'We have a bottomless purse' were this legal panjandrum's actual words. They did at first have the intended effect on Paul, whom I was meeting unobtrusively at the home of mutual friends, and he told me he simply could not justify spending so much company money on a battle in London that I had warned he was likely to lose.

The next time we conferred, a few weeks later, he was a client transformed. He giggled as he told me of a personal message from the prime minister, delivered by a somewhat down-at-heel Tory MP, to the effect that despite all his charitable works, Paul would not be elevated to the House of Lords – so Helen his wife would not become a Lady – if he published *Spycatcher*. Paul, a former refugee from the Nazis, treated these threats with highly amused contempt and spent a small part of his fortune preparing for publication outside the UK's jurisdiction, in Australia.

The Thatcher government, foolishly thinking that country to be still a colony, despatched its cabinet secretary to Australia to give evidence for an injunction based on the British Official Secrets Act. On his way, the stuffed-shirt Sir Robert Armstrong assaulted a press photographer and when settled in the witness box had to admit to being 'economical with the truth'. The Australian judge, unlike his pliant English brethren who were granting injunctions left, right and centre against newspapers that were publishing snippets from the book, rejected the government's claim. Its appeal was roundly dismissed by the Australian High Court on the basic English law principle (which should have been obvious to the Treasury solicitor and his QCs who were conducting this lawfare) that independent countries do not enforce the penal law of foreign nations.

Spycatcher was published in Australia, then in America and Europe, but still the most senior British judges insisted on banning it in Britain – earning their depiction on the front page of the *Daily Mirror* under the headline 'YOU FOOLS'. The *Sunday Times* was finally able to publish after a decisive judgment from the European Court of Human Rights, and as a result of all the publicity Paul Hamlyn was able to sell over a million copies of a not very good book. After Labour came to power in 1997, he would be given the peerage he well deserved, taking as his motto 'There must be another way'. But the government had the last laugh: its supine Parliament changed the Official Secrets Act to extinguish finally any prospect of free speech by members of the security service: they go straight to prison if they open their mouths, even on their deathbeds. They have no defence that they acted in the public interest.

In a nation largely bereft of great cases or constitutional guarantees, we have few explanations, other than from Milton, of the rationale for free speech. The best we have done is to borrow. The 1998 Human Rights Act enshrines in UK law Article 10 of the European Convention, which declares that the right to freedom of expression 'shall include freedom to hold opinions and to receive and impart information and ideas without interference by public authority and regardless of frontiers'. But Article 10 goes on to list exceptions 'necessary in a democratic society' – and there are a lot of them: national security, public safety, the prevention of disorder or crime, the protection of health or morals or the reputation or rights of others, disclosure of confidential information and maintaining the authority of judges. At least these exceptions only apply if they are 'necessary in a democratic society' – the criterion upon which all cases must turn, and which only allows restrictions that answer a 'pressing social need'.

At first blush, this seems a reasonable and reasoned presumption in favour of free speech unless an exception can be proved necessary in a free society. That is how Article 10 of the Convention should be interpreted. It was how Lord Scarman, the fine judge who was its leading advocate, predicted it would be interpreted, but he was wrong. Judges have insisted that thanks to the Convention's Article 8 right to respect for privacy, the exceptions are of equal weight and deserve to be 'balanced' against free speech rather than proved exceptional. Nonetheless, the Convention does link the value of freedom of expression to that of democracy – a form of government which necessarily carries with it the right of all citizens to speak and write and work out how to vote. The Australian High Court decided similarly that although Australia had no freedom of expression guarantee in its constitution, the very fact that the document provided for democratic government inevitably meant that such a guarantee must be implied into it – certainly for speech that concerns politics and government. The

UK's third Royal Commission on the Press, chaired by Lord McGregor and reporting in 1977, came to much the same conclusion:

> We define freedom of the press as that degree of freedom from restraint which is essential to enable proprietors, editors and journalists to advance the public interest by publishing the facts and opinions without which a democratic electorate cannot make responsible judgements.

Anchoring freedom of expression in democratic government is a necessary, but not sufficient, rationale: the Australian 'implication', and European case law, give more latitude to the media in coverage of politicians than of businesspeople, who usually wield more power, as do influencers of various kinds who operate alongside government or below its waterline. If there is a genuine public interest in investigating a non-political public figure of any kind, or a corporation, it is difficult to understand why the test should be different. There was a good deal of self-satisfaction in Western democracies when it turned out that the doctor in Wuhan who first detected Covid, and raised alarm by emails to colleagues, had been visited by political police and warned to keep quiet. But the same results could have been achieved to silence whistleblowers in the UK, bound by the Official

Secrets Act in government laboratories or by non-disclosure agreements if working for private companies, or in public hospitals and threatened with breach of confidence actions if they reveal company or management secrets. The mere fact that a country is democratic is no guarantee that its people are free to speak their minds or to access important information. That depends on its media laws.

There has been little interest in Britain in developing a philosophy of free speech, and little advance since Milton, and later John Stuart Mill. University law schools and bar schools disgracefully ignore it, and uncritically teach defamation law as a small part of courses in torts. As for judges, they may pick up an understanding of free speech from their own reading, but are heavily recruited from commercial law practices in which it does not feature other than as a way of stopping employees from breaching non-disclosure agreements. There is 'judge school', to which all judges are summoned for occasional weekends of training, but in seventeen years of attendance, as a recorder, I never heard a lecture about media freedom or even the 'open justice principle', which all judges must apply but frequently do not.

There have been a few distinguished jurists in the past fifty years who have understood free speech and tried to develop the law in its favour – I would rate Denning (although never against overblown claims of national security), Scarman, Bingham, Alan Rodger, Hoffmann, Hale and Jonathan Sumption, but on the evidence of the ZXC case, none of the present members of our Supreme Court. They would, however, loyally apply statute law, if only it were clearly and effectively directed to favour free speech.

Living in a democracy that allows citizens to express themselves can be a boon to their psychological well-being, although the UK (unlike most European countries) does not afford them an enforceable right to reply when attacked. It should – the best cure for abuse of speech is more speech. Steam can be let off in a tweet, but social media is controlled by profit-seeking private providers which regulate themselves and may censor views they dislike, although few of their victims have much that is worthwhile to tweet in 280 characters. Blogsites carry opinions of more pith and moment, but can make conspiracy theories and disinformation seem credible. New laws are needed to regulate electronic dissemination of so-called information, and 'online safety' bills and the like are on their way, beyond the scope of this book. But new media is subject to old laws, with the defects that attend their application to print journalism and broadcasting.

The lies that wing around the world on Facebook and Instagram before truth can put its electronic boots on call for revision of that other justification for freedom of expression, that it promotes a 'free marketplace of ideas'. This notion is particularly attractive to liberal American philosophers and its essence may be found in Milton's claim in *Areopagitica*:

> Though all the winds of doctrine were let loose to play upon the earth, so Truth be in the field, we do injuriously by licensing and prohibiting, to misdoubt her strength. Let her and Falsehood grapple; whoever knew Truth put to the worse, in a free and open encounter?

Milton was writing four centuries ago: he might not have been so sanguine about the emergence of truth in a modern English courtroom in which falsity has all the funds or where laws relating to privacy and confidentiality are designed to suppress inconvenient facts. The purpose of defamation should be to nail demonstrable lies, and of privacy laws to leave undisturbed personal matters that are of no business to anyone else. Injunctions, damages and costs should only threaten utterances of little or no public interest, or about people of little consequence (like many so-called celebrities). The main function of free speech is not merely to help people decide how to vote, but to open their eyes to the reality of how power is exercised before and after they do.

That is why it is insufficient to regard free speech as an attribute of a democracy which can be 'balanced against other values of equal weight'. It is not merely a way of holding politicians and governments to account for their deficiencies: it is a force for finding out and exposing the injustices and inequities that exist in spite of those deficiencies. We know for a fact that in all capitalist countries the gap between the rich and the not-so-rich is widening by the year, that corporate power has increased, that tax avoidance shades into tax evasion and that privileges for the wealthy have exacerbated inequalities in health and education. The function of investigative journalism is to report, analyse and comment on such matters, and on the beneficiaries, without let or hindrance. By providing the powerful with weapons to obstruct such examinations, British law reduces the availability of news that is worthy of reporting, precisely because it opens people's eyes to what is happening in their country or their community. For that reason, speech should be accounted the first of our freedoms and have in our laws a presumption in its favour.

3.

Defamation

We need more such serious journalism in this
country and our defamation law should
encourage rather than discourage it.

Brenda Hale*

London is the libel capital of the world, thanks to its
claimant-friendly laws and procedures that tilt the
balance against investigative journalism. It is said that
one of its chief practitioners, Peter Carter-Ruck (his name
always misspelled by *Private Eye*), went to Moscow at the
turn of the century to explain the advantages of British
law to its oligarchs. They could always win in Russia by
bribing the judges, but no one would give the verdict
much credit. They could never win in America, thanks to
the First Amendment. So to London they came, to Court

---

* *Jameel v. Wall Street Journal Europe* (2006) UKHL 44, para 150,
[2007] 1AC 359.

13 of the High Court of Justice in the Strand – suing American newspapers that had exposed their questionable dealings. First came a banker named Glouchkov, then a businessman accused of stealing money earmarked to buy shoes for the children of peasants, and then the deeply corrupt Boris Berezovsky, followed in later years by Roman Abramovich and other oligarchs.

As a general rule, they could invest a few million to acquire a 'golden passport', stash their wives in Chelsea mansions, their mistresses in Mayfair, their children at Eton or other public schools, hire a distant member of the royal family and donate to the Conservative Party. Then they would have enough connections to claim a 'reputation' in England that could be damaged, even if the story was entirely about their dealings in Russia or had been published in an American newspaper that sold only a handful of copies in the UK. As time passed and internet publication ensued, they would claim additional damages for all the downloads, and add privacy claims to their libel actions. They were men of stupendous wealth, profiteers from the break-up of the Soviet Union and without moral scruple. One of them was fond of leaving messages on the answering machine of my solicitor – the sound of a machine gun, firing.

There had been other foreign plaintiffs, of course. Princess Elizabeth of Toro, for example, Idi Amin's foreign minister whom he had sacked in 1974, he announced, because she had been found performing oral sex in a toilet at Paris's Orly airport. This preposterous statement was an early sign of his madness and so was reported by all national newspapers. All were forced to pay her very large damages and apologise profusely – the 'repetition rule' meant that they were directly responsible for any news story they repeated from another published source.

There were Americans, too, seeking to vindicate a reputation they could not protect at home because of the First Amendment. I recall wrong-footing the Texas oilman Oscar Wyatt – on whom J.R. Ewing's character in *Dallas* was based – who claimed he had a reputation to protect in England because his son had committed adultery with the Duchess of York and he had dined at Buckingham Palace (indeed he had, but only because the Queen was away). In 1992 I was called as an expert witness in New York on the oppressiveness of English libel laws, during an attempt to enforce an English libel judgment for damages. To do so, ruled the judge, would be 'antithetical to the First Amendment', not only because English newspapers had at the time no public interest defence, but because defendants were forced (and, of course, still are) to bear the burden of proving that their books or articles are true.

The Burden of Proof

Oligarch claimants are so rich that they do not need libel damages – what they really want (but will never admit) is to chill any investigations into their corrupt conduct. My most principled American clients, like the *Wall Street Journal* and *Forbes* magazine, had the money to fight them, but the difficulties of satisfying the burden of proof in relation to stories set in Russia was very often impossible. The journalists believed, on reasonable grounds, that they were true, but sources feared reprisals and would not come forward, while information was either unavailable or was only obtainable by paying bribes. I recall traipsing through the snow at Red Square, with Mark Stephens and our American lawyer colleagues, Bob Sack and Stuart Karle, hunting for evidence to defend the *Wall Street Journal* against oligarch libel claims. We were offered everything we asked for, even KGB records, but at a price and by shady characters who could not have withstood cross-examination. In an English courtroom, evidence from Russia even about Russia would have been regarded as tainted, however true.

Boris Berezovsky, ex-KGB, made his billions by profiting from his corrupt links with Boris Yeltsin, and was an oligarch with a 'roof' (that is, a protection squad) of murderous Chechens. He had been investigated by a conscientious journalist from *Forbes*, Paul Klebnikov, who became a friend as well as a client. Klebnikov had enough evidence to meet the burden of proving corruption, but could not prove, although he reasonably suspected, that Berezovsky had ordered at least one murder.

The case was entirely Moscow-centric, and *Forbes* sold few copies in England, but that is where it was ordered to stand trial by a narrow decision of the Law Lords that Britain should be a libel globocop, resolving cases for the wealthy of the world who could claim some small connection with it.* The case was finally settled in a deal with no damages. Shortly afterwards, Paul was assassinated on a street in Moscow by a Chechen hit squad. Whether Berezovsky had ordered a revenge killing, nobody knows. He fell out with Putin, and was later found dead in his Berkshire mansion. It looked, or had been made to look, like suicide, but nobody, including the coroner, could be sure. Where oligarchs are concerned, court proceedings rarely get at the truth, especially in libel cases when the burden of proving it rests on the defence, and at inquests into their sudden deaths.

Nonetheless, when investigative journalism gets sued for libel, that burden always falls on the journalist, whether he or she chooses to defend on the basis of its substantial truth or on the basis that there was enough

---

* *Berezovsky* [2000] UKHL 25.

evidence of its truth to make its publication a matter of public interest. That was the task I undertook for Bill Browder, an American businessman in Moscow whose lawyer, Sergei Magnitsky, had exposed a complicated fraud: crooked police and tax officials had 'captured' Bill's companies and used them to embezzle $230 million of public money. Incredibly (although not incredibly in Russia) Magnitsky was arrested by the very police he had accused, and was later beaten to death in jail.

Unable to obtain justice in Moscow, Bill made some videos about the crime and was sued by one of its alleged perpetrators. This was not an oligarch – just a police officer with an annual salary of £15,000. But he hired very expensive London lawyers and counsel, and hunkered down for a six-month trial that would have cost him millions. I had prepared what was probably London's longest libel defence, almost book length, in an attempt to satisfy the burden of proof, but the case was thrown out on the grounds that the police officer had no reputation in England. It left me wondering which part of the Russian state had stumped up the millions to bankroll him.

Although truth is a defence, proving it in court may be impossible and there are crippling legal costs (according to *The Lawyer* magazine, senior solicitors acting in these cases for oligarchs charge up to £1,500 an hour). It may be difficult to prepare a full-blooded counter-attack:

witnesses may have died or disappeared, or been promised confidentiality. Difficulties of this kind mean that many true statements are not published or if they are, soon become the subject of apologies rather than defences. To repeat: the burden of proof rule in respect of the defence of 'truth' in defamation comes from that archaic presumption that every defamatory statement is false, for no better reason than that it is defamatory. As defamation means no more than 'lowering the claimant in the estimation of right thinking people', this presumption is absurd – many such statements are in fact true. But the media, as defendant, must prove them true. Not beyond reasonable doubt, but close to it, because courts insist that 'the more serious the allegation, the more cogent the evidence required to prove it'. All that claimants need to prove is merely that the words about them are seriously defamatory and that they were published by the defendant. Then the burden of proving truth, or any other defence (such as an honest opinion or public interest) shifts to the defendant.

In the first place, this is unprincipled and illogical. It stands to reason that those who come to court seeking damages should be required to establish the essence of their claim, and this is the requirement in every other civil law action. The essence of a defamation claim is that the words are false. Second, in the cases that matter concerning investigative journalism, proof to a high standard may well be impossible, because confidential sources relied on for the story will fear reprisals and decline to give evidence, or may be discounted because they are sleazy or have criminal convictions. There have been notable miscarriages of justice: as we have seen, Profumo won damages for the suggestion that he had slept with Keeler,* and Tour-winning cyclist Lance Armstrong won large damages for drug allegations that he admitted ten years later. The closet-gay pianist Liberace won huge damages over what readers might insinuate from a critic's description of him in the *Daily Mirror* as a 'winking, sniggering, snuggling, chromium-plated, scent-impregnated, luminous, quivering, giggling, fruit-flavoured mincing, ice-covered heap of mother love'. All of which he was, as well as gay – the imputation for which he won his damages.

In 1993 the *New Statesman* published the fact that Prime Minister John Major was widely (and correctly) rumoured to have a mistress. He had campaigned on 'family values' and the story was convulsing Westminster, so the magazine was prepared to defend its report as substantially true. However, Major sued its distributors, W.H. Smith, who immediately paid him a very large sum in damages. Years later, it turned out that the sting of the

---

* See Geoffrey Robertson, *Stephen Ward Was Innocent, OK* (Biteback, 2013), pp. 33–41.

story was true – the prime minister was having an affair, not with the rumoured Downing Street caterer, but with his cabinet minister Edwina Currie. He would not have won damages had the truth been known (although the caterer might, had she sued, for the serious libel that she had willingly had sex with John Major). The cowardly W.H. Smith settlement conveniently covered up a relationship that would have been seen as hypocritical, and to add insult to injury the *New Statesman* was contractually forced to reimburse W.H. Smith for the damages and costs the distributor had paid to the undeserving politician.

Jack ('Slipper of the Yard') Slipper, the keystone cop who failed to bring the great train robber Ronnie Biggs back from Brazil, won large damages and had a book (*Slip Up*) by Anthony Delano pulped, after the Foreign Office refused to disclose evidence needed to confirm Slipper's incompetence. When it became available, the detective was dead and his estate – with its libel winnings – had been distributed.

The burden of proof proved fatal to the *Sun* newspaper, which in 2001 exposed the corruption of former Liverpool goalkeeper Bruce Grobbelaar: the jury was undecided about his denial and so the paper could not meet the high burden of proving corruption. The Law Lords, however, examined the evidence and declared the verdict perverse, reducing his £85,000 jackpot to a derisory £1.* Had Grobbelaar borne the burden of proof, he would not have won the unjust verdict and the scandal would probably not have come to court in the first place.

The list of miscarriages of justice, due in large part to the burden of proof placed on media defendants, goes on and on (and see Jeffrey Archer's perjured victory, pp. 117–18). Usually unseen are the many occasions when substantially true allegations are not allowed to be published, by media lawyers who advise that there is a risk of losing millions in costs and damages if they cannot be proved – the most egregious example being the failure to expose Jimmy Savile (p. 30).

There is an ironical aspect to the unfair burden of proof – it may induce utterly unmeritorious claimants to sue for libel. This was illustrated in 2022 by a case that made the High Court look low. It was brought by Rebecca Vardy (a footballer's wife) against another such 'WAG', Coleen Rooney, who had defamed her by publishing an inference, based on Rooney's own detective work, that Vardy had betrayed her trust by being the source of confidential information which had appeared in the *Sun*. After a number of preliminary hearings which whetted the public appetite and ran up costs (Vardy's silk was being paid £10,000 a day, reported *The Times*, while Rooney's somewhat younger champion was charging

---

* *Grobbelaar v. News Group Newspapers Ltd* (2001) 2 All ER 437.

only £8,000), there followed a week-long trial. This produced a 290-paragraph judgment concluding that 'Wagatha Christie' had most likely fingered the correct suspect. The case featured extensively in all newspapers but Ms Vardy, who had brought it, cut a most disconsolate figure during her two days in the witness box. Its main interest, at least for those 'in the business' was – given the evidence – how on earth Vardy had come to think that she had any prospect of success. Her very expensive and very experienced lawyers may simply have thought that the burden of proof would be too heavy for Rooney to surmount – her detective work had turned up no 'smoking gun', although the judge concluded that this would have been found on the telephone of Vardy's agent who had providentially dropped it in the North Sea. The case may serve as a warning to those with more money than sense who are minded to take advantage of a claimant-friendly libel law to suppress the truth, but they will only be deterred if their alleged libeller is wealthy enough to stump up a few million pounds in legal fees to shoulder the burden of proving that truth. Rooney, who was, recovered £1.7 million of her legal costs from Vardy, an up-to-date measure of the expense of lawfare in defending a simple case.

The Public Interest

The two reasons why US courts refused to enforce English libel judgments were that in English law the burden of proof is on the media and that at the time there was no 'public interest' defence. In the US, the latter is secured under the First Amendment by permitting any critical allegation about a public figure, unless it is made maliciously, or recklessly in relation to its truth. European human rights law similarly allows the media greater latitude for critical comments about politicians and the powerful. But in Britain, entire books on politics have had to be pulped and reprinted if a particular passage was deemed defamatory, and news stories on matters of public concern could be the subject of litigation if they included a defamatory claim that the journalist reasonably believed to be true at the time the story was published but that subsequently turned out to be mistaken, or incapable of corroboration.

It was not until the twenty-first century that British judges were prepared to develop a public interest defence, tentatively for the *Sunday Times* when sued by the Irish prime minister and then for the *Wall Street Journal* when it reported, in the wake of 9/11, an important international story about Saudi Arabia's collaboration with the CIA in monitoring leading Saudi businessmen

– including the claimant, Mohammed Jameel (see pp. 74–5). The *Journal* could not prove the story in court, because it derived from confidential CIA and diplomatic sources, but its public interest was such that the Law Lords set aside the verdict against the publication, which had been upheld by the Court of Appeal, and declared that defamation law should be reshaped to encourage serious journalism.

The very notion of a public interest defence for investigative journalism was long resisted by common law judges, who kept asking how it could ever be in the public interest to publish untruths. The answer is not found in the portentous claim that journalists write 'the first draft of history' – like most first drafts, they may well require substantial revision. The case was better put by Sir Harold Evans, explaining that journalism was a 'search for the truth' – and in that search, on matters of public interest, wrong paths may be followed, clues may lead nowhere and smoke may billow not from a fire but from a smoke machine. What matters, for free speech, is that the law protects important statements that are reasonably believed to be true at the time they are made – so long as they are retracted if and when they turn out to be untrue. For this reason, while Arron Banks was entitled to sue Carole Cadwalladr over her defamatory TED Talk, when the truth emerged after a public inquiry (partly provoked by her allegations) and she dropped the claim that they were true, so his pursuit of her should have ended, or at least have been entertained by the courts no longer, because he had already been exonerated and no longer needed a remedy.

There is now a much-touted statutory public interest defence to libel actions, but Parliament in the 2013 Defamation Act did not think to require claimants to disprove it: the burden of proof is, as always, on the defence. It can, moreover, prove for journalists a snare and delusion. The defence requires proof that the journalist's own belief in the public interest of his or her story was reasonable, and judges have ordered them to disclose their notebooks, iPhones and laptops, discussions with contacts, their electronic messaging and so on. Not only is this time-consuming and invasive, but it gives claimants out for revenge the opportunity to discover journalists' working methods and their sources of information.

The defence should have been predicated on the reasonableness of the asserted public interest rather than the subjective belief of the journalist. In order to raise it, the journalist is forced into the witness box for lengthy cross-examination about working practices and information sources. Carole Cadwalladr and other journalist defendants have spoken movingly about the strain on themselves and their families in the lead-up to trial, and then she was kept in the witness box for three days' intense cross-examination of her work.

Public interest may be raised as an argument to resist injunctions and lawsuits for breaches of confidence or misuse of private information, but always with the burden on the defence, as it is with the public interest defence in the Data Protection Act. This amounts to a comprehensive disrespect for the media's Fourth Estate or 'watchdog' duty to expose wrongdoing: never has Parliament or the judiciary provided it with a presumption in its favour. In British courtrooms, the media must always be on the defensive, its worth always to be proved and never to be presumed.

Damages and Legal Costs

The right to damages for defamation began as an alternative to the duel as a remedy for personal insult, but in 1894 a court extended this right to a corporation – the South Hetton Coal Company. It was an illogical extension, since companies have no feelings capable of injury, and in any event their directors and employees retain the right to sue over any slur on the company which can be connected to their work for it. But a corporation as claimant carries more weight, and its writs have a chilling effect because of the 'bottomless purse' that can fund the fight all the way to the Supreme Court.

Corporate abuse of the power to sue for defamation was epitomised by the McLibel action, brought to crush protests by two penniless activists, whose badly printed leaflets casting aspersions on the fast food giant's burgers would have been thrown away had this exorbitant action not come to feature on the websites of the world. After the longest trial in English legal history, which lasted for 313 court days and provided a transcript of 20,000 pages, together with 40,000 pages of documentary evidence and 130 witnesses, the multinational was awarded damages of £60,000, which the unemployed defendants could not pay. The Court of Appeal hearing lasted twenty-three days, and the farcical proceedings only ended after nine and a half years when the House of Lords refused leave to appeal. The European Court a few years later condemned the entire spectacle, both as a disproportionate suppression of free speech and an unfair trial, ranging the silks retained by the corporation against two unrepresented protestors.* Nothing of any worth came of it, other than to feather the cap of a young barrister who had given free advice to the impoverished defendants and taken

---

* *Steel and Morris v. UK* (2005) 41 EHRR 22, and see John Vidal, *McLibel: Burger Culture on Trial* (Macmillan, 1997).

them successfully into Europe – Keir Starmer made his first mark.

I made an attempt to overturn the South Hetton precedent in the subsequent case of *Jameel v. Wall Street Europe*, but narrowly failed, two judicial votes against three, with Judge Brenda Hale pointing out that the precedent had been decided 'before we were a proper democracy', by which I took her to mean, before women were accorded the vote or allowed to be judges. This would have been a useful way of dispensing with unenlightened nineteenth-century precedents, but South Hetton was allowed to live on in the law reports until the 2013 Defamation Act, which allows trading corporations to sue only if the defamation is 'likely to cause the body serious financial loss'. This would rule out the damage from the fifty ill-printed pamphlets in the McLibel case, but it is not much of an improvement – corporate lawyers and accountants are quick to predict drops in share prices or fall-off in customer numbers, or increases in the cost of borrowings, or loss of management time in replying to the libels, so public companies may continue to harass their critics with defamation actions. Due regard for free speech requires abolition of the power of corporations to sue for libel – a reform that has been achieved in Australia and New Zealand, unless the company employs fewer than ten people.

It took assistance from the European Court to reform the law of damages for defamation, which were hitherto unrestrained. A jury awarded a massive £1.5 million to Lord Aldington, accused (with some, but not sufficient, evidence) in a book by Count Tolstoy of being involved in the decision at the end of the Second World War to send Cossack prisoners back to Stalin, who predictably had them all executed. Elton John had been the first to make a million, to compensate for some tabloid squib, and Jeffrey Archer had won half a million for the claim, for which there was almost but not quite enough admissible evidence, that he had sex with a prostitute, to whom he had paid £2,000.

Damages of this dimension were disproportionate, the European Court ruled, and as a result they have now been scaled down, to a current maximum of £300,000. Even so, damages for injury to reputation tend to be more than the law awards for the loss of an arm or a leg, and more than the Criminal Compensation Board awards to those who have suffered grievous bodily harm or even rape. In 2021, for a brief social media spat about Jeremy Corbyn, his defender had to pay £35,000 in libel damages, and the price of her own and her adversaries' legal costs, which came to £1 million.

That is now the real problem – damages are dwarfed by legal costs. The going rate for KCs is heading towards £1,000 an hour, with a fashion accessory – a junior – at up to two-thirds of the price. Then come the solicitors – a team of partners, employed solicitors, paralegals and clerks, whose bill is much higher. For oligarchs, of course, this is chickenfeed, but for authors and small magazines it can be fatal, and big media groups often do not fight, even when they have a good case, if the claimant is a powerful corporation or a billionaire bent on revenge. Newspapers, book publishers, authors and broadcasters all know that the cost of fighting an action – even if it takes only a week in court – will cost both sides over £1 million, which the loser will have to pay. (It was estimated that the Johnny Depp libel case against the *Sun* in 2020 cost him £10 million, and he had to pay the newspaper's costs of £5 million.)

Even if the media side wins, it usually does not get back the full amount – that needs an order for what is termed 'indemnity costs', which covers about 90 per cent. The winner receives only about 70 per cent, because 'normal' legal costs are assessed at what is reasonable, rather than at what is billed. It never occurs to judges that if a claimant loses against a publisher, that means they have attempted to infringe its freedom of speech and deserve to have indemnity costs awarded against them. Otherwise, the successful publisher will be seriously out of pocket. Bill Browder beat the Russian state – or whatever organ of it bankrolled the policeman who sued him – but was left, after his victory, to pick up a bill of £500,000.

The costs problem has been made worse by one well-meaning parliamentary intervention in 1999 – conditional fee arrangements (CFAs) to fund libel actions, for which legal aid is not available. The idea was to help poor people sue the media by attracting lawyers who would take their cases on a 'no-win no-fee' basis, but with a 'win, and double the fee' inducement. This added a new and unpleasant dimension to the game of chance – media defendants could be mulcted for twice as much if they fight and lose against CFA lawyers greedy for their 'success fee' and hence prepared to try every trick in the book – the 1,503-page libel bible, *Gatley on Libel and Slander* (a snip at £349) – in order to win. That is how the CFA regime, intended for the poor, came to be exploited by the rich. Naomi Campbell, the wealthy model, sued with a CFA. She won damages of only £3,500 for breach of her privacy, but her lawyer's costs amounted to £250,000. These were doubled to £500,000 to provide her lawyers with their 'success fee'.

Our top judges declined to stop lawyers for the rich taking new cases on CFAs, although they expressed disquiet and called for a 'legislative solution', which in 2018 at least abolished the 'success fee' but left claimant lawyers to recover their 'normal' fees if they won – which is success enough. They can also recover any insurance premium they have taken out should they lose – this often costs a six-figure sum, which if they win must be shouldered by the defendant. We should submit applicants for CFAs to a stringent means test, or better still abolish them, and allow legal aid to be extended to libel cases certified as reasonable, where demonstrable and serious lies have been published by media organisations that have refused to retract them, about victims who lack the large amount of money necessary to take them to court.

Defamation turns the Temple of the Law into a casino. Each case that goes to trial, after various pre-trial reviews and appeals to decide on meanings and disclosure, is an elaborate gamble. The defendant must decide how much to 'pay into court' and when. If a sum of money is paid into court by the defendant, the claimant may take it and the case ends. If not, and the claimant presses on and wins, but no more than the amount that has been paid in, the claimant must foot the entire bill. On the other hand, if the defendant so demolishes the claimant's character that he is awarded the libel raspberry ('the lowest coin in the realm'), the defendant will be saddled with the entire costs if he has failed to make a 'payment in' of a penny or more.

A much-publicised case of the 1970s was brought by a colonel with a penchant for spanking the young ladies whom he lured through the small ads in *Private Eye*. Because a newspaper had exaggerated his perversions, but not by much, he was awarded a derisory half-penny.

The paper had not had the foresight to 'pay in' a penny, so it was saddled with the costs of the entire trial. In 1998 the *Coronation Street* actor Bill Roache sued the *Sun* for suggesting that he was as boring in real life as the character he played in the show. The paper 'paid in' £50,000, which he thought insufficient for this dreadful slight, and graspingly pressed on to win more – but the verdict was precisely £50,000, so he had to pay his own legal costs, which were twice as much.* Judges are kept in the dark about any 'payment in' – the envelope is opened only after the damages have been announced. It's the justice game show moment, and should be televised.

The costs are so high – of trial and then appeal to the Court of Appeal and then, if allowed, to the Supreme Court – that few media organisations can afford them. It is no coincidence that the greatest victory of recent times for free speech in Britain was won by Americans, in the form of the *Wall Street Journal*. After losing at trial and in the Court of Appeal, the *Journal* found some judges in the House of Lords in 2006 who actually understood the importance of free speech in the public interest, and fashioned a defence for it. The case concerned Mohammed Jameel, a billionaire Saudi businessman, owner of Hartwell Motors in Oxford and Toyota dealers in the Middle East. In the aftermath of 9/11, with its

---

* *Roache v. News Group Newspapers Ltd* (1998) EMLR 161.

mainly Saudi aeroplane hijackers, there were serious doubts over whether that country would join the international crackdown on terrorist financing. The *Journal*'s reporters, investigating in Jeddah and Washington, discovered that it would: at the request of the CIA, the kingdom was actually investigating leading Saudi businessmen. To show that they were in fact leading, it named them. When Jameel and his company sued, English judges at trial and appeal simply could not understand why it was necessary, for the public interest, to identify him – he should have been hidden behind a cover such as 'a prominent Saudi business identity'.

It took Lord Hoffmann to explain that the crucial element of news value attached to identifying the large and respectable business entities was to show that cooperation with the US Treasury was real and not confined to a few fringe companies. 'To convey this message, inclusion of the names was necessary', because it made the public interest point of the story – in effect, its 'newsworthiness'.*

London's claimant-friendly law has not only attracted 'libel tourism' from foreign dignitaries seeking to protect their international reputations, but has caused publishers to remove from editions published in the UK material that

---

* *Jameel v. Wall Street Journal Europe* (2006) UKHL 44.

is available elsewhere. Twenty-two changes were made to *Sideshow* – William Shawcross's indictment of Nixon's aggression in Cambodia – before it could be safely published in Britain, and *Time* magazine removed from its European edition Daniel Moynihan's joke about Henry Kissinger – 'Henry doesn't lie because it's in his interests. He lies because it's in his nature' – lest the worthy Dr should take them to Court 13. No one dared to publish in England Kitty Kelley's 1997 bestseller, *The Royals*, which hinted at more scandals in the English aristocracy.

The 2013 Defamation Act unaccountably did not deter the worst form of 'libel tourism', namely where foreign claimants – oligarchs and the like – hire lawyers to sue British publishers in the High Court. It did address a minor problem: if the defendant publisher is foreign, the claimant (whether foreign or not) must show that England is clearly the most appropriate place for the action, but this does not apply to foreigners who sue English-based publishers over stories that concern events that take place abroad and require overseas investigations and evidence. Such cases are really unfit for trial here, because they concern foreign events and are extraordinarily difficult and expensive to investigate. They are often brought by oligarchs, but the courts will not generally strike them out.

As for kleptocrats and foreigners who have been formally sanctioned by the UK government, the sanction should deprive them of the right to bring any action in England, because they no longer have a reputation here. Why should foreign individuals or corporations sanctioned for war crimes or serious human rights abuses be allowed to use our courts in order to win money and discourage reporting about their crimes? Incredibly, the Sanctions Act (2018) expressly permits them to do so, by exempting money sent to the UK to pay fees for 'genuine legal advice and litigation'.

In the first month of Putin's war on Ukraine, his most odious sanctioned oligarch Yevgeny Prigozhin ('Putin's chef') continued his libel action against Eliot Higgins, founder of the investigative website Bellingcat, who had published evidence of Prigozhin's connection with the Wagner Group, Russia's brutal mercenaries. It took four more weeks of bombing before Prigozhin's law firm asked to be discharged, without being required to pay Higgins' costs, but the Sanctions Act should have prevented them from suing on behalf of a sanctioned oligarch in the first place.

British judges can be ludicrously accommodating to foreign libel litigants. When the film director Roman Polanski had to testify – he was the claimant in a 2005 libel case against *Vanity Fair* magazine – they were told he could not come to England, for the very good (but truly bad) reason that he would be arrested for the rape of a thirteen-year-old girl, a crime for which he had been convicted in California, and instead of attending court for sentence he fled to his native France. The British Law Lords kindly permitted him to give evidence from his five-star Paris hotel, with his own make-up artist on hand to powder his face.*

Individuals should be able to stop, and obtain damages against, those who tell reckless or deliberate lies about them. That is why we need a law of libel and slander, so long as it does not prevent the exposure of wrongdoing. But in British newsrooms, libel is a major inhibition on free speech, as the pre-action letters arrive from lawyers to the wealthy, laced with pompous demands for suppression or retraction. It will often amount to high-paid bluff, but failure to call it is the consequence of unconscionably high costs and the business caution of media insurers. Or in-house lawyers who fear the evidence may fall just short of compelling, because the sources fear reprisals from employers or from the government whose guilty secrets they have divulged in breach of contract or data protection law or reasonable expectation of privacy.

Nonetheless, for all the problems the law presents, victory remains possible and many publishers who succumb to fears about costs might achieve it if they

---

* *Polanski* [2005] UKHL 10.

fought on. But this can take courage. When Parliament, disgracefully, amended the Bill of Rights to allow Neil Hamilton to continue his libel action, the *Guardian* executives were so worried that they asked my advice about their chances. I had to tell them they were not high. Our one witness, Mohamed al-Fayed, had been branded a liar by a Department of Trade and Industry report, and our best argument – that another minister also accused of taking 'cash for questions' had confessed to Parliament and resigned – could not be mentioned to the jury because the Bill of Rights prevented evidence of anything said in Parliament.

The *Guardian* put on a brave face – its reputation had been put at stake by Hamilton's boasts he would smash them, and I demanded more journalists and forensic accountants and a junior, Heather Rogers (now a sought-after silk) at a cut rate – only £250 an hour. They had no choice but to agree, and I went to see al-Fayed to beg him to help. It was the week before the trial, and Hamilton and his co-claimant, the Tory PR agent Ian Greer, were told by their lawyers that they had a 90 per cent chance of success. That would put us at 10 per cent, but a certain camaraderie developed between the lawyers and journalists and we never lost confidence.

A few days before trial came the breakthrough – Alison and Iris, two unimpeachable witnesses, secretaries who had meticulously noted Hamilton's importunities on their telephone records. 'Neil wants his envelope' was the code to prepare a brown envelope stuffed with £2,500 of al-Fayed's cash, an inducement for Hamilton to ask questions in his interests.His lawyers withdrew, so he threw in the towel, confronted the next day with his picture splashed on the front page of the *Guardian*, captioned in large letters 'A LIAR AND A CHEAT', followed by pages of evidence of Tory sleaze (some eight MPs had their snouts in the Harrods trough). It propelled the demise of John Major's government, blasted by corruption, but it demonstrated that defamation cases can be won – with lots of fortitude and funding.* The paper's editor Alan Rusbridger needed those qualities again when sued by Jonathan Aitken, who raised what he called 'the sword of truth' – a libel writ – against the *Guardian*. He was giving evidence when the sword disembowelled him: a *Guardian* journalist discovered an incriminating document in a hotel basement in Austria, and this lying claimant was in due course jailed for perjury.

The threats inherent in lawfare are not confined to costs: journalists speak of the psychological toll that is taken by answering aggressive legal letters and preparing for unpleasant cross-examination in the witness box. As

---

* See David Leigh and Ed Vulliamy, *Sleaze: The Corruption of Parliament* (4th Estate, 1997).

noted, some have been subjected to surveillance and other forms of attack from the public relations firms, unconstrained by codes of conduct, hired by wealthy adversaries, and who sometimes engage security firms, also without ethical constraints, made up of former police officers and ex-employees of MI5 and GCHQ. The great irony is that claimants, whether individuals or corporations, can claim their legal fees and public relations costs as 'business expenses' incurred in protecting their reputations, and hence tax deductible courtesy of HMRC.

For all that Britain boasts about free speech, it has had a wretched history here – other countries do it better. American law gives much surer protection to defamatory words if they are published in good faith about public figures, and most European laws treat defamation as no big deal, providing a right of reply for those attacked or else an order for retraction, rather than heavy costs and damages. It has been estimated that the cost of obtaining a remedy at trial for wrongful publication in Italy and France amounts on average to €15,000, whereas in the UK it is very often in excess of £1 million. Perhaps it is the English way to have an almost supernatural belief in the importance of reputation (notwithstanding Iago's point that it is 'oft got without merit and lost without deserving'), and hence to devote much precious court time to forensic struggles over the meaning of words and the extent to which evidence can be extracted from foreign countries.

There is no question that the law should deal with demonstrable falsehoods – those who can demonstrate they have been demonised should be entitled to come to court and obtain a 'declaration of falsity'. A 'right of reply' law would not infringe freedom of speech – it would cure an abuse of speech by ordering more speech. But the problem in many contested cases – especially those brought by oligarchs and multinationals – is that the courtroom is not necessarily a place for discovering the truth. Witnesses can lie convincingly or refuse to attend, documents may be lost and rules of evidence (especially those that exclude hearsay) may not permit the full picture to emerge.

Occasionally, of course, forensic methods can make a breakthrough. I was witness to one such occasion, when I dropped in to Court 13 to witness a much-publicised libel action brought by a South African woman named Jani Allan, who had sued over reports that she had sex – with fascist boer politician Eugene Terre'Blanche – on the top of the Voortrekker Monument in Pretoria. Ms Allan came to London and collected large libel damages from all the local media, who could not surmount the burden of proving this outrageous libel. But there was one exception: Channel 4, then commanded by Michael Grade, who hired George Carman to cross-examine

Allan. I arrived for a front-row seat just as Jani had finished a carefully rehearsed examination-in-chief by her counsel, Charles Antony St John Gray, an urbane fixture of the libel bar.

George began in his florid, Rumpole-like way: 'Are you sitting comfortably, Ms Allan? Are you sure? Of course you have told my Lord and the members of the jury that you would never commit adultery ...' At this point, Charles turned to whisper derisively to his junior, 'A typical Old Bailey hack.' While his back was turned, George produced a small dog-eared book from beneath his gown, delivered to him mysteriously the previous night, and had it shown to the witness. 'Will you look at this entry in your diary, please Ms Allan? It describes, does it not, in lurid detail, a sexual bout you had – with a Captain Ricardo, of Alitalia Airlines?' The words 'Captain Ricardo' and 'Alitalia' were given an emphasis redolent of the distaste that would no doubt be shared by a middle-class English jury. Charles jumped to his feet – this was an improper ambush – and called for an adjournment.

Outside the court, George chain-smoked while his admirers congratulated him on this *coup de théâtre*, Michael Grade declaring it more dramatic than anything on Channel 4. Ms Allan withdrew her action, although I doubt whether she paid back her other libel winnings. Disporting herself with Captain Ricardo did not logically mean that she had done so with Terre'Blanche. However, there is much to be said for Grade's insight that libel actions should be televised – the claimants could not complain, as they want public vindication, and defendants who raise the public interest defence could hardly protest that the public would not be interested. The Ministry of Justice might sell the rights to recoup the costs of court time – the lengthy Johnny Depp stoush with the *Sun* over Amber Heard would have been widely watched, as it was in the UK when the equivalent trial in America was televised, and if ever Meghan goes into the witness box against the *Daily Mail* ...

There was once, centuries ago, a libel action brought by a plaintiff over a handbill that implied he was a highwayman. The evidence in the case proved that he was in fact a highwayman, and the judge ordered him to be taken out of court and hanged. Few libel actions today end quite so satisfactorily for the defence.

4.

Privacy

'Such as listen under walls or windows, or the
eaves of a house, to hearken unto discourse, and
thereupon to frame slanderous and mischievous
tales, are a common nuisance ... and are
punishable ...'

Thus read England's first privacy law, in 1360. The village
Murdoch was put in the stocks and pelted with rotten
eggs. The tradition lapsed, until judges in Naomi
Campbell's case in 2005 refashioned, with the help of
Article 8 of the European Convention, a new law against
invading anyone's 'reasonable expectation of privacy'.
Until then, eavesdropping had been a tabloid sport. The
world chortled at the future king of Britain, intercepted
on the telephone wishing he were a tampon inside
Camilla, and at actually hearing, on a 'premium rate'
telephone line, cabinet minister David Mellor (at the
time, in charge of media regulation) making love to an
out-of-work actress. Princess Diana (aka 'Squidgy') was

taped by a retired bank manager, Cyril Reenan, whose hobby was eavesdropping on other people's conversations: he insisted he did not want to hurt the royal family, so he delivered the tapes to a tabloid for safekeeping.

This was the era, in the 1990s, when the judges lost patience with the press. The most senior of them demanded a privacy law after a journalist and photographer sneaked into the intensive care hospital room of *'Allo 'Allo!* star Gordon Kaye, and interviewed him as he came round from brain surgery.* The judges lamented that they could give no remedy for this 'monstrous invasion of privacy', so it is little surprise that they seized the opportunity when Article 8 entered English law a few years later. What had riled them was the behaviour of the tabloids, but when the time came to make a law, they did so mindless of its danger to investigative journalists.

Media proprietors had cynically attempted to stave off the advent of a privacy law by funding 'voluntary self-regulation' in the form of the Press Council. This was a confidence trick which in time failed to inspire confidence. When the Press Council condemned the *People* for publishing a picture of the Duke of York's naked baby daughter, the newspaper responded by publishing a picture of the naked Duke of York and invited its readers to vote in a telephone poll over whether the photos were

---

* *Kaye v. Robertson* [1990] EWCA Civ 21.

offensive. The Press Council severely reprimanded the *Sun* for taking telephoto pictures of Princess Diana on a private beach, so the paper published a grandiose apology, which it illustrated by reprinting the very same pictures, under the banner headline 'THIS IS WHAT THE ROW'S ALL ABOUT, FOLKS'. Down at the Old Bailey, it was noticed that the crime of blackmail had virtually disappeared, as those privy to scandal no longer demanded money from the victim, but simply sold the secret to a tabloid newspaper.

One long-time impediment to investigative journalism has come from the law of breach of confidence, which enables the grant of an injunction to stop publication of information obtained from confidential relationships. This was the basis of the lawfare against *Spycatcher* – the author was bound to eternal silence by his contract of employment with MI5. The Thatcher government injuncted all secret service memoirs, including *One Girl's War*, a Mills and Boon-style account of how a debutante working in MI5 during the war fell in love with her boss, only to find her romantic hopes dashed by the dawning realisation that he was happier in the arms of men. (When the government sued to stop the book's publication in Ireland, its case for doing so was laughed out of court.) The previous Labour government had even sought to stop publication of Richard Crossman's diaries, on the basis that cabinet ministers owed a duty of secrecy forever after they had left government. The lord chief justice found the book boring (Crossman had been Harold Wilson's minister for housing) and allowed the *Sunday Times* to serialise it on the basis that cabinet confidentiality lasted only ten years.

The legal eminence who stamped his prejudices on the law of confidentiality in this period was Lord Denning, a judge (Master of the Rolls, 1962–82) of great erudition and a somewhat florid prose style, with a ferocious middle-class morality. He believed strongly in the aphorism of equity, that 'there can be no confidence in iniquity', by which he included tax avoidance and sex outside marriage. It was not to be covered up – on the contrary, the press had every right to expose the indulgences of celebrities like Tom Jones and John Lennon, to show why, as he thought, they should not be celebrated. And although Denning was an English nationalist who always upheld the government on national security – his 1976 decision that it could deport American journalist Mark Hosenball without any evidence, merely for asking questions about GCHQ, was quoted approvingly by prosecutors in the repressive countries throughout the Commonwealth – he did not much like fascists, and refused to stop the *Sunday Times* from publishing a story about the junta in Greece that was based on information purloined from their public relations advisers in London.

Denning's moralistic approach to the law of confidence has fallen out of fashion – he would never have found for Naomi Campbell and probably turned in his grave at Max Mosley winning £60,000 for the *News of the World* revealing his penchant for spanking orgies – but his judgments do serve to underline just how subjective is the test of whether there is 'a reasonable expectation of privacy', and if so, whether there is a public interest in invading it.

This can be demonstrated by a case brought by the *Top of the Pops* presenter Jamie Theakston to stop the *Sunday People* from revealing that he had visited a brothel.* The question was whether a man who frequented such an establishment could have a reasonable expectation of confidentiality. The judge decided that he could not, although perhaps another judge who had visited brothels would have decided differently. A few years later, Max Mosley was allowed a reasonable expectation of privacy at his orgy – did it make a difference that he had arranged it himself?

Judicial answers to such questions inevitably depend on individual values – the judge in Theakston did ban publication of photographs, on the grounds that a man does at least have a reasonable expectation, when he goes to a brothel, that there will be no cameras. The

---

* See *Theakston v. MGN Ltd* (2002) EWHC 137.

Sunday People attempted a public interest defence, with a humbug argument (based on Denning) that it had a right to show a man respectable enough to present a BBC programme for young people as a person who pays for sex, and the court actually bought this in relation to Theakston's attendance, but not in respect of the photographs. It made the distinction (it always does, in this class of case) between legitimate public interest and that which merely interests the public. Judges do not realise that sometimes it may be both.

For example, the distinction is always applied to injunct 'kiss and tell' (usually 'kiss and sell') stories by women who have been attached to wealthy men with whom they have fallen out, often for good reason because of abuse and ill-treatment. Judges are kind people usually, and so prevent publication on the grounds that the revelation will traumatise the man's wife and upset his children. But does a woman, badly or unconscionably treated in a clandestine relationship, not have freedom of speech – freedom, even, to speak to the *Sun*? Far more seriously, judges still enforce confidentiality imposed by 'non-disclosure agreements' (NDAs), even though it is well known how they cover up abuse or sexual harassment by powerful men. It took Zelda Perkins, assistant to Harvey Weinstein, years before courageously determining to breach the NDA imposed by his solicitors and to reveal how he had attempted to rape her co-worker.

There is a certain sexism at play at some injunction hearings – unexamined affidavits from the celebrated but anonymous man or his lawyers, hasty or lawyer-less responses, if any, by the woman, and an almost knee-jerk grant of the application by a (usually) male judge. MeToo is not a movement much noticed by the higher judiciary.

If we are serious about privacy cases, perhaps we should bring back the jury to decide them in a way which reflects the world and not the rarefied atmosphere of the Inns of Court. It was once the famous boast of Professor Dicey – the oracle of our unwritten constitution – that freedom of speech was safe in England so long as trial by jury survived – but now it has been abandoned for libel and has never been allowed for privacy and breach of confidence. Judges impose their own ethical values on the media, but they do not understand how investigative journalism works – its lifeblood comes from 'leaks' and tip-offs – and their worldly wisdom is open to question. Whether a man caught in a brothel is entitled by law to keep this quiet, or a billionaire who hired women for a spanking session should be paid damages by a newspaper which exposes him, are questions that only a representative sample of the public can answer according to contemporary standards. Of course juries take more time and are more expensive, but a publisher should be entitled, if it wishes, to have their verdict – at its own expense if its public interest defence fails.

A jury may well have decided that Mr ZXC, a very wealthy US national suspected of committing serious corruption offences, had no reasonable expectation of secrecy over the fact that the police were seeking information about him from an overseas court, and that this was a matter of real public interest. They are not trusted to make these decisions. But each jury verdict would be a popular precedent, a warning to the wealthy, on the one hand, and a 'mind how you go' to the tabloids on the other, that an ethical red line can be drawn, and where currently to locate it.

Nobody much listens to IPSO, the press regulator, not only because it is paid for by proprietors and has no teeth, but because the decisions of its committee – of the self-opinionated 'good' and the slightly great – are not a genuine test of public opinion. A recent adjudication was that a first-person story by writer Lynn Barber, about the problems with a refugee she took in to her home, should not have been published despite being of significant public interest. It clearly was, and it is questionable whether a jury would have condemned its publication. But now it is the values and the prejudices of judges that will decide whether Article 8 – the public interest in protecting privacy – will overbalance Article 10 – the public interest in freedom of expression. The public, through its representatives on a jury, can have no say in this decision about where its interests lie.

This balancing act is now a feature of every privacy case, once the judge has decided that there is a reasonable expectation of privacy and the media defendant claims a public interest in publishing. This has come as a surprise to many who urged incorporation of the European Convention: its most powerful supporter, Lord Scarman, insisted that the right guaranteed by Article 10(1) would prevail, unless the claimant could show that an Article 10(2) exception, such as 'protection of the reputation and rights of others', necessarily overruled it. Strasbourg case law insists that exceptions must be narrowly construed, and that the guaranteed right must prevail unless its restriction is 'necessary in a democratic society' to answer to a 'pressing social need'. Scarman was correct, but what he did not envisage was that Article 8, which called merely for 'respect' for home and correspondence, would be elevated to a general right to reputation of equal weight to free speech.

This came about by an illegitimate shift in Strasbourg jurisprudence: the drafters of the Convention had deliberately omitted from Article 8 any protection for 'honour and reputation', and left the latter as a subsidiary right under Article 10(2) that should only prevail in cases of necessity.* This was the approach the European Court

---

* See Geoffrey Robertson and Andrew Nicol, *Media Law*, 5th edn (Thomson, 2007) para 2-19; 5-18.

took in the *Sunday Times* Thalidomide case, where it rejected the UK government argument about 'balancing' rights, and said that Article 10 did not call for a balance at all: it established a right to free speech to which there are limited exceptions and the burden is on those seeking to restrict the right to prove that the particular interference with it is necessary. But thanks to a confused and actually wrong decision by the European Court in Princess Caroline's case (protecting her public shopping trips by suggesting that Article 8 could help her personality development), the British Law Lords were soon declaring that Article 8 protected 'reputation' and that 'neither article has precedence as such over the other'.* From that point – 2005 – the judges had their thumbs on the scales of justice, and they have never been removed.

Parliament has made one attempt to help by adding to the Human Rights Act a section – 12(4) – which directs the judge to have 'particular regard to the Convention right to freedom of expression'. But as the Ministry of Justice has conceded, section 12(4) has not had any great effect on the way judges have determined such

---

* Lord Steyn in Re S (2004) UKHL 47, para 17. This disastrous decision was made without argument: both counsel agreed it and the judges did not bother to examine it, but the balancing act has been adopted ever since.

issues.* It is not a defence and is often brushed aside when they grant injunctions to stop publication until trial (often a year or more away) when interest in the news will be less and so the trial will often be abandoned by the newspaper defendant. Judges grant these suppression orders whenever they think the claimant is more likely than not to succeed, although at a hurried interim hearing without witnesses and without a detailed defence, it is doubtful that they can make more than a knee-jerk judgment. Judicial knees generally jerk in favour of privacy, certainly if the claimant relies on breach of confidence, which may have come about through a leak by employees bound by non-disclosure agreements in their contracts. One simple way of curing the problems caused by the balancing act between Articles 8 and 10 would be to amend section 12(4) of the Human Rights Act to provide that 'publication cases' must be dealt with under Article 10 – a presumption in favour of free speech rather than a balance – with Article 8 thus becoming an exception to rebut that presumption only if it could be proved 'necessary in a democratic society'.

The problem for the media is that many if not most of its truly newsworthy revelations are based on informa-

---

* Ministry of Justice, Human Rights Act Reform (CP 588, December 2021) and see p. 113 for the government's plans to abolish this slim need of public interest.

tion provided by sources who are in breach of privacy or confidentiality, and hence the story is likely to be injuncted by an employer if they know beforehand that the information has leaked. The newspaper or broadcaster will not want to alert them, so instead of inviting comment from the party whose document is about to be revealed – which is usually good practice in the interests of fairness – the newspaper will publish as soon as possible. The journalist will keep fingers crossed that the story will be so important – or so politically embarrassing – that available legal action will not be availed of.

This was the case in 2022 with news that the wife of the then UK chancellor was a non-dom who'd saved hundreds of millions in tax by opting for that status. She had a reasonable, indeed overwhelming, expectation of privacy over her tax affairs and could have obtained an injunction had she been tipped off about what must have been an unauthorised leak by someone at HMRC. Instead, post-publication, she had to face the political music, and reacted to the public outrage by renouncing her non-domiciled status. ZXC, however, learned that Bloomberg had the confidential information before it was published, and was able to act quickly so as to prevent this. There are few rich people who these days are disposed to echo the Duke of Wellington – 'publish and be damned' – when damnation, at least by an injunction and costs, is available to stop publication.

Privacy actions are an excellent vehicle for lawfare, because they cover up the truth, whereas defamation claims focus on statements alleged to be untrue. In defamation there is less scope for an injunction, which will not be granted if the defendant proposes to try to prove the truth of his statement, but privacy claims can readily win an injunction until a trial, which may never go ahead. Moreover they have this advantage for lawfare – they can be brought up to six years after publication, so oligarchs can bide their time before launching an attack. In defamation, action must be brought within a year, but when Parliament laid down this time limit they did not bother to apply it to other media laws. These particularly favour oligarchs and rich businesspeople: as the five Supreme Court judges said in the *ZXC v. Bloomberg* case, letting slip their bias in favour of the wealthy: 'Ordinarily we would anticipate greater damage to a businessperson actively involved in the affairs of a large public company than to a private individual.'*

Privacy cases go unnoticed in the court lists, with 'alphabet soup' titles like *X v. Y* or *ZXC*, and the media can be banned from reporting the very existence of the action by way of a super-injunction. The only way to breach this court order without going to jail is if an MP or peer hears of it and identifies the case under parliamen-

---

* *Bloomberg LP v. ZXC* (p. 140).

tary privilege, as Lord Hain did in 2018 by revealing that Sir Philip Green had obtained an injunction to stop the *Daily Telegraph* from reporting allegations that he had sexually harassed and racially abused his staff. Hain was criticised, especially by judges, for using his privilege to disobey their orders, but most of the public thought that he was right. As Enoch Powell once pointed out, 'What is the use of this privilege, unless it is used?'

It is likely that 'misuse of private information' actions will increase after the green light given to using them to suppress news about corruption allegations in ZXC's case. That involved information given to Bloomberg in what the court assumed (no doubt correctly) was a serious breach of confidence, and it ruled that the general public interest in keeping confidences outweighed the public interest in free speech about combatting corruption, or at least in discovering how it was being combatted. In its public interest balancing act, the court found a heavier public interest in keeping confidences than in revealing corruption, even in a company that had been accused, in Parliament, over many years of being involved in wrongdoing. The Supreme Court judges did not seem to value the media's watchdog role in reporting corruption: it was mentioned only to make the point that Bloomberg had done no more than to report the law-enforcement action. This is true – but there is no indication that the decision would have been different had

Bloomberg dug up some evidence on its own initiative. The court dismissively commented, 'We do not consider that the nature of the activity in which the claimant was engaged is a factor of particular significance.' Most would see the question of whether that activity was corrupt as being of great significance. The court held, for the circular reason that there was a greater public interest in keeping confidences than in reporting the fight against corruption, that Mr ZXC was entitled to suppress details not only of the reasonable suspicions of a law-enforcement agency, but also of his own identity, although he had been previously mentioned by name in debates in Parliament.

Its lengthy judgment was mainly devoted to establishing that henceforth those suspected of crime by police and other law-enforcement authorities have a 'reasonable expectation of privacy', even after they have been arrested, at least until they have been charged (which may take some time) and appear in open court. This is yet another development which prevents the 'watchdog' press from watching how police perform and from barking – that is, alerting the public – when they do so unlawfully or incompetently (as Operation Midland officers did in misleading a court to obtain warrants to search the homes of Lords Bramall and Brittan and former MP Harvey Proctor – it was not until Proctor breached his own right to privacy and complained publicly about the police that anyone had an inkling of how badly the police were behaving). It prevents press freedom from actually assisting law enforcement, because publication of the names of suspects sometimes causes witnesses to come forward, not only to provide evidence to incriminate them further, but sometimes to help their defence.

A very recent example was provided by the conviction for sexual assault of a fifteen-year-old boy by Conservative MP Imran Ahmad Khan. The politician had initially succeeded in keeping his name out of the papers, arguing that he was a strict Ahmadi Muslim and his life would be at risk if it were to become known that he was gay and fond of gin and tonics (and, allegedly, teenage boys). Newspapers, unusually, made common cause and appealed this gag order, which was lifted by the High Court. But after his conviction, as a result of the publicity, a witness came forward to tell police that he had suffered a similar assault from Khan when he was sixteen.* Had Khan's name been released earlier, this allegation might have been added to his charge sheet.

The Supreme Court decision in ZXC's case has made it much more difficult to argue that the public interest outweighs the right to privacy. The court declared that there is a 'general public interest in the observance of

---

* See 'MP Tried to Gag Press', *The Times*, 12 April 2022.

duties of confidence' which 'strengthens the justification for interfering or restricting the right to freedom of expression'. This means that, in respect of all the news-worthy stories based on 'leaks' from employees or involving personal data or 'confidential' documents, their very confidentiality will weigh heavily in the judi-cial balance against publication, because courts place such value on employment contracts, even if breaking them would help to reveal 'iniquity' such as sexual abuse.

The case is a striking example of the lack of support for press freedom at the top level of the current judiciary, and regrettable because its line of reasoning must hence-forth be applied as a precedent for all future cases. It was factually the worst possible example for a test case, because Bloomberg journalists had not added anything to the story by way of investigation and its editors had not thought about the privacy implications before publishing. It might, strategically, have been better for the media if they had not taken it on appeal to the Supreme Court, because as a result of this judgment other publishers with better cases will not challenge the suppression of important stories based (as many are) on breaches of confidence.

It was a test case and the current Supreme Court judges failed the test. Hard cases make bad law, and this case very soon influenced the decision by Scotland Yard to withhold the names of all persons issued with fixed penalty notice fines for breaching Covid health regulations by attending parties in Downing Street. Home Office 'media guidance' decreed that 'the identities of people dealt with by fixed penalties should not be released or confirmed', so that the public would have no idea which ministers and public servants had, for personal pleasure, broken a law – their own – which most citizens had made sacrifices in order to obey. The public interest in publishing their names was obvious – to see whether those who broke the law had played a part in creating it. When Downing Street owned up to the prime minister having been fined, public outrage was an emphatic rebuttal of the notion that there could be no public interest in revealing the identities of the subjects of police powers.

Still more rods are fashioned for the backs of investigative journalists, and particularly of their sources, under the pretext of protecting privacy. The latest is the Data Protection Act of 2018, which enables publishers to be sued for 'processing' (that is, publishing) personal data, broadly defined as 'any information relating to an identified or identifiable living individual'. There are some exemptions for media, but not enough – in privacy cases, civil claims for breaches of the Data Protection Act, and even of the European General Data Protection Regulation, now regularly appear on the statement of claim for damages against newspapers and broadcasters. These damages usually run merely to five figures, and are dwarfed by legal costs, but they are providing new opportunities for clients of lawfare firms to harass their enemies. Section 170 of the DPA makes it a criminal offence, punishable by a fine of up to £10,000, knowingly to disclose personal data 'without the consent of the controller', who will simply be an official in the relevant company or organisation which has a guilty secret that has been leaked by a whistleblower.

Section 170 may not be used against journalists, but it will certainly be used to trap and to persecute their sources: the UK's Information Commissioner has a large office staffed with investigators and lawyers with police powers of search and seizure (no need for a court order), and the ability to interrogate under caution and to prosecute after any 'leak' that embarrasses the government or an employer, no matter how important the information that is leaked. There is a weak public interest defence – the burden of proving it, of course, being placed on the defendant. It is as if the discredited section 2 of the Official Secrets Act* has been revived and held over the head of every employee, civil servant or professional

---

* Which prohibited any public servants or government contractors revealing information they acquired in the course of their jobs – reporting, for example, the number of cups of tea served on a given day in the Ministry of Defence canteen.

who is privy to 'personal data' that touches upon or demonstrates a matter of scandal and concern.

There was no fuss when the Data Protection Act passed through Parliament – perhaps MPs and their researchers did not bother to read as far as section 170. But it is a prime example of what Richard Crossman called 'the British disease' of secrecy, a weapon to wield if needed to punish anyone who embarrasses 'great men of the realm' such as Matt Hancock (the Information Commissioner's Office raided the homes of those suspected of leaking CCTV footage of his tryst in breach of Covid regulations); and the government may have had in mind, or in hindsight, intimidating sources of the kind who in 2009 passed on to the *Daily Telegraph* the 'personal data' of MPs who had so abused (some criminally) their personal expense claims. Yet again, a law that chills investigative journalism, this time by deterring public-spirited people who disclose information of public importance to the media, threatening them with a trial and a criminal record. Parliament did not debate section 170, and the media itself and none of its investigative journalists bothered to lobby against it or report on its dangers, for all their ethical codes that require the protection of sources.

If section 170 prosecutions get underway and succeed, journalistic sources will start to dry up, which means there will be even less serious journalism. That is because the right to protect sources is fundamental to investigative journalism. It was never acknowledged until a young journalist named Bill Goodwin, his fine for contempt of court by not disclosing his source upheld unanimously by judges in the High Court, took his case to Strasbourg in 1996, and the Eurocourt ruled against the UK. It explained:

> Protection of journalistic sources is one of the basic conditions for press freedom ... Without such protection, sources may be deterred from assisting the press in informing the public on matters of public interest. As a result the vital public watchdog role of the press may be undermined and the ability of the press to provide accurate and reliable information may be adversely affected ... such a measure cannot be compatible with Article 10 of the Convention unless it is justified by an overriding requirement in the public interest.*

This had never occurred to British judges before. Their common law decreed that journalists who disobeyed court orders to name their sources were guilty of criminal contempt. In 1983 the *Guardian* had been

---

* *Goodwin v. UK* (1996) 22 EHRR 124 at para 39.

forced to identify its source for a scoop about US cruise missiles being sent to Greenham Common, and their whistleblower – a young employee of the Ministry of Defence named Sarah Tisdall – was sent to prison. After *Goodwin v. UK*, journalists have been protected. But their sources are not, if uncovered by independent police inquiries or by their employers or by statutory bodies like the Information Commissioner's Office. They can be prosecuted, or sued for damages, even though they were assisting 'the vital public watchdog role of the press'.

5.

Reform?

Lords and Commons of England, consider what
nation it is whereof ye are: a nation not slow and
dull, but of a quick, ingenious and piercing spirit.
It must not be shackled or restricted. Give me the
liberty to know, to utter and to argue freely
according to conscience, above all liberties.

Milton, *Areopagitica*

On 22 June 2022, the Johnson government published
what it variously called a 'British' or 'Modern' Bill of
Rights, for the Lords and Commons to consider. Although
its purpose was to cut back, quite severely, the right to
challenge the government over human rights abuses, it
was introduced by the minister – Dominic Raab – and
the Ministry of Justice with a press release fanfare that its
intention was to 'strengthen protection for freedom of
speech'. The press fell for this lie, with even *The Times*

editorially proclaiming the benefit of a bill 'which contains explicit measures to protect free speech'. Quite the contrary: had its journalists read the small print, they might have realised that the bill does precisely the opposite. Nonetheless, it advanced to the stage of second reading when the Truss regime suddenly withdrew it, and withdrew Mr Raab, without explanation. It remains on the table, its fate dependent on the musical chairs of the Tory ministry. Within a few weeks, Raab was reinstated as justice secretary in the Sunak government, and he soon announced that his bill would return as well.

The Conservative Party had been promising a 'British' Bill of Rights in its manifestos ever since the 2010 election, and set up a commission on the subject in 2012. It reported that the Human Rights Act (1998), introduced by the Blair government to make the European Convention part of British law, was perceived by press and public as too 'European' – but it did not agree on a substitute.

The 'modern' bill introduced in 2022 was not a Bill of Rights at all – it reduced the rights set out in the Human Rights Act, and made them difficult to enforce by introducing new application and permission procedures, carefully designed to prevent many human rights cases from being brought to court. The government said nothing about this real purpose, but instead insisted that its object was 'to strengthen protection for freedom of speech'. This was propaganda, but interesting propaganda because editors were naïve enough to believe it, thus demonstrating the vulnerability of media freedom when those in the media cannot even recognise the danger when it stares them in the face.

This chapter will refute Mr Raab's bogus rhetoric that the bill enhances freedom of speech, and then consider some legislative reforms that would in reality do so.

This Bill of Rights begins deceptively – section 4(1) directs courts to give 'great weight to the importance of protecting freedom of speech'. But which courts, exactly? Read on (which journalists failed to do), to discover that this so-called protection will not apply in the courts that really matter, where the right will have little or no weight at all. Section 4(3) says 'This section does not apply ...' to four classes of case: (a) criminal proceedings or rules; (b) proceedings involving questions of privacy; (c) citizenship, deportation; and (d) national security.

(a) Criminal Proceedings

Criminal proceedings are those in which editors, journalists and sources obviously need free speech. A few years ago, quite a few were prosecuted over dealings with police or other officials, and most were acquitted after arguments over their free speech rights. No longer will these resound with any weight if this bill is passed. Nor can they be raised in defence of journalists charged with contempt of court, which is a criminal offence. Our statutes and our common law are studded with offences that can be charged against journalists, or their sources. If this bill receives parliamentary approval, it will apply to all criminal proceedings and rules of police conduct – including challenges to searches and seizures of journalistic material. Far from 'strengthening' the protection of free speech, removing it from prosecutions of journalists weakens it seriously.

(b) Privacy and Breach of Confidence

To proceedings involving questions of privacy and breach of confidence, these cases are henceforth to be determined without giving any or any great weight to freedom of speech, because 'obligations of confidence' arising from any agreement – employment, marriage, government service – are not to be questioned by considerations of the public's right to know. This includes 'non-disclosure agreements' (NDAs) – the preferred legal means of silencing women who might complain about sexual assault. Their free speech right will not entitle them to complain to the media or to any public authority. This devious provision (clause 4(3)(b) in the bill) means that courts will continue to grant injunctions to the wealthy and powerful, without paying attention to any right of the media to expose their operations. Such actions – for breach of confidence and privacy and data protection – were deployed by Putin's oligarchs for lawfare, and these 'reforms' will make it easier for injunctions to be granted. 'Leaks', as filtered by journalists from their sources, are how significant 'news' gets out: Mr Raab's bill will make such news easier to suppress.

(c) Citizenship, Deportation

The government wishes to prevent free speech arguments being used to challenge its decisions to remove anyone's British citizenship or to deport asylum-seeking dissidents to countries where they might be prosecuted or jailed for speaking out (for example, Rwanda). WikiLeaks founder Julian Assange is currently appealing against extradition on the grounds that it would be a breach of his free speech rights: if this bill becomes law before his appeal is determined, this argument would have little chance of success. Governments have sometimes denied entry to controversial international figures who have been invited to speak to British audiences – their sponsors will not be able to challenge the ban for denying freedom of expression.

(d) National Security

To the determination of any question which may affect national security, not merely is the protection of freedom of expression excluded from Official Secrets Act prosecutions – those alleging espionage or the unauthorised disclosure of official information – but it is removed from any court, civil or criminal, which decides 'any question the determination of which may affect national security'. Only 'may' affect? All that government lawyers need to do is raise the possibility that national security might be affected – in judicial reviews of government action, freedom of information claims, employment tribunals and the like, or other cases where evidence embarrassing to the government or defence agencies may possibly emerge and, 'hey presto', free speech is not a weighty consideration. The government has repeatedly refused to adopt the Law Commission's strong recommendation for a public interest defence to Official Secrets Act prosecutions,* and exclusion of free speech considerations from any case involving national security will prevent any defence for the publisher, no matter how important the revelation.

* * *

* The Law Commission, Protection of Official Data Report, HC 716 (September 2020), p. 245 et seq.

This is the danger of a bill – were it to become an act – withholding any presumption in favour of free speech from so many areas of the law which impact upon the media, thus signalling to the judges that in such cases free speech is not an important value. Mr Raab has claimed credit for 'strengthening' protection for journalists' sources, but all credit for this belongs to the European Court of Human Rights – this bill does no more than attempt to state, quite clumsily and not as well, the law as it has already been declared in *Goodwin v. UK* (see p. 105).

The true deviousness of the government's Bill of Rights can be appreciated from close scrutiny of its section 22, the headnote of which reads: 'Limit on court's power to grant relief that affects freedom of expression'. Headnotes are not used for statutory interpretation, and this section does the very opposite of what the headnote proclaims. It restates, in slightly different words, the test that is already contained in section 12 of the Human Rights Act (which will be abolished once this bill is enacted). It repeats the limit for granting an injunction, which is to say that claimants must satisfy the court that they are likely to succeed at trial in suppressing the story – quite easy, if it is based on information obtained in breach of confidence or a 'reasonable expectation of privacy'. But section 12(4) of the existing Act goes on to impose another test – namely that before banning a publication the court must consider if 'it is, or would be, in the public interest for the material to be published'. And guess what? This public interest 'limit' is not repeated in Raab's Bill of Rights – it will be abolished! In 1998, when the Human Rights Act was being debated in Parliament, section 12(4) was inserted specifically to protect the media, indeed at its insistence, so that the importance of a story could be considered before it could be suppressed. The real malevolence of Mr Raab's attitude towards media freedom may be appreciated by this furtive elimination of the public interest dimension from judges' decisions to ban publication.

There are other aspects of the 'modern' Bill of Rights that will make it difficult for the media to assert its rights to open justice or to obtain information. The government's real purpose is to curtail the rights of everyone to bring human rights claims to court. That includes the press, which will, for example, no longer be able to go directly to the High Court to strike down lower court decisions to ban reporting of a trial, without going through a lengthy and expensive process of obtaining permission and proving that the media would suffer 'significant disadvantage' by any reporting restriction.

The European Convention on Human Rights, adopted into English law by the Human Rights Act of 1998, may be thought too 'European', yet it was inspired by Winston Churchill and drafted by his lord chancellor. Nonetheless, as the 2012 commission reported, the European Convention has failed to induce much sense of 'owner-ship' in Britain (other than by lawyers) – the name itself gives rise to a perception that it is somehow 'alien'. However, this 'British' Bill of Rights proposed by the government is a squalid document in which it is impossi-ble to take any pride, as it is mainly concerned with reducing people's access to justice.

In principle it would be no bad thing to update the Convention – a wonder of its time (it came into effect in 1953), but a time that has passed. There are rights now needed for the disabled, to protect the environment, to be free from disinformation and so on. A 'modern' bill could have the great benefit of teaching children about how this country has contributed so much to the language and content of human rights – by entrenching parliamentary sovereignty, representative government, judicial independence, trial by jury, habeas corpus, the end of torture and so on (if not, alas, freedom of speech). But it would need a preamble set out in language compre-hensible to 'ordinary people' (the patronising phrase used by lawyers to denote anyone who isn't a lawyer) rather than in the legalistic terms of Mr Raab's bill. The previous commission set up by the coalition government in 2012 to advise on the subject mainly comprised a mass of QCs (for which there is no collective noun – a 'purse' of silks, perhaps), so the 'modern' charter is unlikely to capture the language of Shakespeare and Milton, or compare with that of Thomas Jefferson. The drafting of an inspiring 'British' bill should not be left to lawyers, and certainly not to lawyers like Mr Raab – it calls for historians and poets and people with some imagination and literary skill.

How should the law be changed to protect speech, or at least that form of speech that can be described as 'news-worthy' in the sense of being worthy to put before the public for discussion in a democratic society? A lot of litigation turns on tittle-tattle and matters of no great moment – the right to read Meghan's letter to her father, the resolution of a spat between footballers' wives with more money than sense, the detritus of disputes involving 'celebrities' – entertaining for the public, certainly, but the information at stake never much matters. The danger is that legal precedents and 'balancing acts' developed in these trivial cases are carried over and applied to serious journalism – the sort of journalism, as Brenda Hale says, that the law should encourage. If British law is to have a presumption in favour of free speech, the following changes should be made in a law that for too long has had a presumption against it.

Reverse the Burden of Proof

It is an anomaly that in defamation, alone of civil law actions, the burden of proving 'truth' rests on the defence. This is now the reason why American courts will not enforce English libel judgments, because the rule is antipathetic to free speech. It is wrong in principle – those who come to court to claim damages should prove their case. In practice, very often the defendant cannot shoulder the burden if admissible evidence is lacking, because sources afraid of reprisals do not come forward or else it is hidden by offshore tax or trust arrangements or in countries like Russia or Saudi Arabia or Kazakhstan, where crucial information is withheld by governments and impossible to uncover. One very simple amendment to the Defamation Act would help to create a more level forensic playing field, in which claimants would have to prove their claim that defamatory statements about them are untrue. Banking and corporate secrecy in places like Switzerland, Dubai, Malaysia and Russia has left defendants powerless to meet the burden in respect of stories that were probably true and certainly worth investigating. In one uncelebrated case, an experienced Fleet Street editor named Lloyd Turner obtained evidence that Jeffrey Archer had paid £2,000 to a prostitute, so he thought he was safe in venturing to suggest that Archer must have had sex with her, only for a court to hold that Turner failed to satisfy the burden of proof and Archer was awarded libel damages of half a million pounds. When Lloyd Turner later died of a heart attack, he did not have the satisfaction of knowing that Archer would subsequently be jailed for perjury and perverting justice, and would be required to pay his winnings back to the newspaper.

It is remarkable that in a country which boasts of free speech, the media in court must always be on the defensive, bearing the burden of establishing every defence it is permitted to raise. In defamation, that includes the defence of 'honest opinion' and of 'publication on a matter of public interest'. This unfair position is ingrained in legislation: whenever there is a 'defence' of public interest, it is always for the media to prove: in criminal cases (and under the Official Secrets Act, there is not even a public interest defence) and those brought under section 170 of the Data Protection Act as well as civil law, which entitles claimants to injunctions, damages and costs.

End the 'Balancing Act'

In privacy cases, once the claimants have established that they have a 'reasonable expectation of privacy' in the relevant information, the judge performs a balancing act, weighing their Article 8 right to suppress it against the publishers' Article 10 right to freedom of expression. There is no burden of proof to tip the scales and there should be, by way at least of a presumption in favour of free speech unless the privacy claim can be proved to answer a pressing social need. This can be accomplished by a court dealing with the case under Article 10, with its 10(1) declaration and definition of freedom of expression and its 10(2) exceptions to the principle (which include breach of confidence and protection of reputation), exceptions that should be narrowly confined to what is 'necessary in a democratic society'. In other words, in free speech cases Article 8 is irrelevant: it should collapse into the schemata already provided by Article 10. This reform – reversing the judicial lawmaking that began with the seminal Naomi Campbell case and has developed to threaten investigative journalism in the *Bloomberg v. ZXC* decision – could be achieved by an amendment to section 12 of the 1998 Human Rights Act requiring judges to deal with 'publication cases' in accordance with Article 10 alone. In other words, instead of having the public interest in privacy outweigh the free speech claim, as it did in *ZXC*, the court would begin with a presumption in its favour unless satisfied that there was a pressing social need to override it in favour of someone's personal privacy.

No Injunctions on Public Interest Stories

Injunctions are court orders not to publish the information set out in their schedules, and they are almost always obeyed on pain of prison, other than for MPs or Lords when they speak under parliamentary privilege. Lawyers for wealthy potential claimants will rush to court to obtain injunctions, often by telephone from an available judge who will usually grant them without hearing the other side until the next court sitting. The media will not normally be notified and the application is heard 'in chambers' (that is, in secret). Sometimes there will be a super-injunction, which prevents any mention in the press of the case or the parties to it. An injunction against one newspaper automatically binds all others, although they have not had the opportunity to argue against it in court. Claimants must satisfy the court that, at trial, they are likely to establish that publication should not be allowed – a burden that is relatively easy to discharge if the information has come from an 'insider' or by way of any breach of confidence or contract. The law should instead require any claimant for a suppression order to show not merely that they have a reasonable expectation of privacy, but that in addition there is no significant public interest in the information they are asking the court to suppress. This simple amendment should protect serious journalism. It may not save tittle-tattle or 'kiss and tell' features that turn up judicial noses, but in a MeToo era it must be recognised that there is a public interest in allowing women who have been abused by powerful men to tell their story, whether remunerated or not, certainly if they are prepared to attest to its truth. In such cases, judges should drop their simplistic distinction between 'what interests the public' and 'what is in the public interest', by acknowledging that, in the case of women who want to speak out about abuse, it can be both.

Bring Back the Jury

The role of the jury, the 'lamp that shows that freedom lives',* has been hailed as the great protection for freedom of speech. Its historic right to acquit, whatever the

---

* Lord Devlin, *Trial by Jury*, Hamlyn Lectures, 1956 (Revised edn, Stevenson & Co, 1966).

law may be, was memorably extolled in 1885 by Professor A. V. Dicey in his classic work on the constitution:

> Freedom of discussion, is, then, in England little else than the right to write or say anything which a jury, consisting of 12 shopkeepers, think it expedient should be said or written ... Yet nothing has in reality contributed so much to free the press from any control. If a man may publish anything which 12 of his countrymen think is not blameable, it is impossible that the Crown or the Ministry should exert any stringent control over writings in the press ... What is certain is that the practical freedom of the English press arose in great measure from trial of 'press offences' by a jury.*

Dicey was very influential, but in fact completely wrong. The jurors that acquitted John Lilburne and William Penn, and later John Wilkes, are rightly celebrated, but after juries threw out a few sedition cases in the 1790s the government brought them under control by packing them with vetted supporters, 'guinea men' paid if they convicted. Juries loyally sent booksellers to gaol for

---

* A. V. Dicey, *An Introduction to the Study of the Law of the Constitution* (10th edn, Macmillan) pp. 246–51.

distributing Tom Paine's *The Age of Reason*. In Dicey's century they always convicted for blasphemy (even for publishing Shelley's dream-poem 'Queen Mab') and invariably for obscenity, especially the works of 'foreign' writers like Zola and Flaubert.

Only after abolition of the property qualification, and reduction in age limits for jury service, after 1972, do we find juries with much spine. In 1979, the director of public prosecutions announced that he would no longer prosecute the written word following the acquittal of the publisher of *Inside Linda Lovelace*, after the judge had told the jury: 'If anything is obscene, this is.' In 1985, a jury gave the push to the discredited section 2 of the Official Secrets Act by acquitting Clive Ponting, a civil servant who had breached it by leaking documents that falsified government excuses about sinking the *Belgrano*. In 1991, a jury even acquitted two pacifists, Michael Randle and Pat Pottle, on a charge of helping the spy George Blake escape from prison twenty-five years before, despite the prosecution evidence – their new book entitled *How We Freed George Blake – and Why*. The government did not go ahead with the prosecution of Katharine Gun, the GCHQ employee who leaked to the press details of how the UK was illegally bugging the embassies of countries on the UN Security Council thought hostile to the war with Iraq, out of concern that her jury would admire her act of conscience and acquit.

The jury as guarantor of a free press was generally accepted by newspapers in libel actions before 2013: judges had the discretion to stand down juries if the case required a prolonged examination of documents, and even this power was passionately challenged by the editors of *The Times* and the *Guardian*. *Times* editor William Rees-Mogg went to court in person to tell Lord Denning that he could accept no other tribunal in a case where freedom of expression was at stake, and Denning agreed. Then the *Guardian* appealed against the decision to deny it a jury when it was sued by Jonathan Aitken. It had accused him of procuring women for Arab clients, and there were quite a few documents, but the *Guardian* argued that the verdict of a jury would be more credible (and possibly more favourable) than that of a judge. However, the Court of Appeal said that a reasoned decision from a judge would carry more weight than a jury verdict expressed in a few words, so the trial went on before a judge alone (Aitken was caught committing perjury, so it ended). But there was no passion from the newspapers in 2013 – nobody bothered when juries were virtually abolished in the Defamation Bill.

Juries are more likely to find serious journalism to be in the public interest, and more likely to find against oligarchs and other wealthy claimants whose activities may be lawful but nonetheless morally disreputable. Trial advocates talk of a jury having a 'sense of smell' – of odours that may not reach the elevated judicial nose. The prospect of the case being submitted to a jury is certainly a disincentive to some prospective claimants, and I know of cases before 2013 where powerful corporations have for this reason decided not to sue. In defamation, defendants should at least be entitled to elect for trial by jury – it is a historic right which was thoughtlessly taken away.

A jury verdict is more publicly acceptable than a decision by a single judge, and the reasons for the jury decision, while not elaborated, will be fairly clear from the trial itself. It would be useful to have juries in privacy cases – I doubt whether they would have compensated Naomi Campbell for being photographed in a public street, especially when entering Narcotics Anonymous after proclaiming that she never used drugs. There must be doubt whether a jury would have awarded Max Mosley £60,000 for the revelation of his predilection for spanking orgies. If they had (and juries may well find against sensational newspapers in privacy cases), the verdicts would help to draw lines about what is publicly acceptable, because they are perceived as verdicts representative of the public opinion. There have never been juries in breach of confidence or privacy cases, but it would be a satisfactory tribunal to decide what amounts to 'a reasonable expectation of privacy' and the issue of whether publication would be in the public interest. If juries are the 'lamp that shows that freedom lives', why not let them illuminate media freedom?

End Corporate Power to Sue

Defamation and privacy are essentially remedies for personal pain and suffering and for loss of reputation or integrity. There is no compelling reason why this human right should belong to a non-human artificial entity. The Defamation Act limits serious harm, in the case of trading companies, to criticisms 'likely to cause the body serious financial loss', but this formula allows corporations to threaten and bring actions, with speculative evidence that share prices may tumble or that customers may go elsewhere, or in cases where defamation makes borrowing and raising capital more expensive. The threat of being sued by a large corporation can be chilling in itself. The right to do so is not appropriate for non-human entities and it is not necessary – any defamation of a company will usually be defamatory of its CEO and other executives, who retain the right to bring an action. For reasons suggested earlier (see p. 69), the UK should adopt the Australian law that denies the right to sue for defamation to companies that have more than ten employees, and a similar restriction should be placed on corporate actions for 'misuse of personal data' – because it is personal. The right to bring a privacy action should be confined to the human being whose data has been misused.

End Libel Tourism

Oligarchs, kleptocrats and multinationals flock to London, the libel capital of the world, to burnish reputations they cannot protect at home, for three main reasons: (i) English media law is the most claimant-friendly; (ii) English court decisions in claimants' favour have much higher standing than any they would obtain from corrupt courts at home; and (iii) to intimidate critics, especially human rights and anti-corruption NGOs, that are mostly based in London. The first reason is the fault of the law, the second a matter for some pride, and the third is objectionable, especially when it threatens to close down small charities doing their best to spotlight corruption in distant countries.

The government said it would stop libel tourism in the 2013 Defamation Act, but it did not. It merely made it hard for claimants – oligarchs, kleptocrats, multinationals from wherever – to sue people who are not 'domiciled' in Britain or Europe. This protects a few foreign newspapers that are circulated here, without having sufficient residence or offices to be 'domiciled'. It does not withdraw the courts' jurisdiction from cases brought by foreigners, relating wholly or mainly to their foreign operations, against English publishers. Thus Abramovich and his fellow oligarchs, and the Russian gas giant, were welcomed to sue Catherine Belton and HarperCollins over a book the facts of which were only accessible, if at all, in Russia. The libel courts cost the country a lot, and there is no reason why their services should be extended to foreign tourists unless the dispute is closely connected to this country and the court can obtain access to the evidence necessary to resolve it.

SLAPPS

It is a very good idea for those threatened with a defamation or privacy claim over a public interest publication to have a quick path to a court empowered to strike it out. Anti-SLAPP laws work in the US because all the judge has to do is to rule out actions that infringe First Amendment protections. But they will not work that way in Britain, for the reason Lord Scarman pointed out to *Private Eye* when Sir James Goldsmith, determined to close the magazine, sued all its distributors and newsagents:

> Neither wealth nor power entitles a man to
> censor the press. If, however, his purpose be to
> vindicate and protect his reputation, the use of
> all remedies offered by the law for that purpose
> cannot be an abuse of the court's process ...*

The rich, in other words, are perfectly entitled to spend their millions to win damages they do not need from defendants who cannot afford to fight. If, however, there were to be amendments of the kind suggested in this book – a reversal of the burden of proof and public interest defences for serious journalism that a claimant had to disprove – then it would make sense to have a fast-track procedure to nip unmeritorious claims in the bud. The particular strategy deployed by Goldsmith and Maxwell – of suing newsagents and booksellers and forcing them to stop selling the offending publication – has been ended by the 2013 Act, which confines actions in defamation (but not privacy) to authors, editors and publishers. It should have added proprietors. (I once sued Rupert Murdoch personally, on behalf of Michael Foot, whom the *Sunday Times* accused of being a KGB spy. He settled fairly quickly for a six-figure sum in damages.) Another libel pest, the 'vexatious litigant' – exemplified in the past by

---

* *Goldsmith v. Sperrings* and various distributors [1977] 1 WLR 478, and see Richard Ingrams, *Goldenballs* (Deutsch, 1979).

the Church of Scientology – can be stopped, but only if they have lost previous cases and try to re-fight them by actions against others. At least the government would have no difficulty in principle from adding a ban on using English courts to the sanctions it is imposing for war crimes and human rights abuse (currently, on several hundred wealthy Russians). As well as cancelling their entry visas and seizing their assets, it could simply disqualify them from taking any action in British courts. The existing sanctions expressly allow them to do so, and to bring in money to pay their lawyers. Preventing fees being paid to lawyers would be a surefire way to stop litigation.

Recognition of how oligarchs and their lawyers have been able to harass and embarrass authors and investigative journalists has called forth demands for an anti-SLAPP law – taken seriously by the Ministry of Justice in 2022 which issued a consultation paper on the subject. The first problem was how to define a SLAPP. Mr Raab described it as an action 'where the primary objective is to harass, intimidate and financially and psychologically exhaust one's opponent via improper means'. But this 'primary purpose' will be impossible to prove – how can solicitors' letters, required by the pre-action protocol, be called 'improper' when they demand redress for a libel? It might be possible to craft a law, applicable to all claimants and all cases, that gives a wider meaning to 'abuse of process' and entitles a judge to strike out an otherwise good claim if it is 'inappropriate to be tried' because, for example, it invokes foreign facts or transactions that cannot be scrutinised by admissible evidence in a London courtroom, or the claimant has refused offers of other remedies (mediation or recourse to IPSO), or there is a stark 'inequality of arms' (for example, the McLibel case), or a trial would be disproportionate or would not settle the quarrel. These are some of the factors identified in a model law which the anti-SLAPP Coalition is promoting, with widespread support from media figures, although judges would be reluctant to use it (for Lord Scarman's reason, above) and its complexities will make more money for reputation lawyers (and more still, when decisions under it go to appeal). This 'model law' does nothing to remedy the defects in the present law.

Just as questions of meaning and disclosure are settled pre-trial, so 'serious harm' could be tested and a broad discretion given to the judge to stop a trial that can serve no purpose – as in the case brought by Arron Banks who had already been exonerated. However, it would be futile to have an anti-SLAPP law based on having to prove that the claimant's 'primary objective' was to intimidate journalists – that is a consequence of the present law, but claimants will always say, 'I have suffered serious harm and my primary objective is to obtain a remedy to which the law entitles me.' They cannot be denied access to the law simply because the consequence of the case will be to intimidate journalists. The best answer is to reform the law so they will not succeed.

The Costs Nightmare

In a free market profession, legal fees are as high as the market will stand, and both sides in hard-fought litigation will be faced with having to pay the other side's bills if they lose. And even if they win, it's not a case of 'winner take all' – they will normally be given an order for 'normal' or standard costs, which will total about 70 per cent of their outlay (for Bill Browder, who had the libel action against him thrown out because it was inappropriate for trial in England, the costs he still had to pay amounted to £500,000). An order for 'indemnity costs' would give a successful defendant about 90 per cent, and such an order seems appropriate whenever a publisher has beaten off a libel or privacy claim – by definition, in these circumstances, the action is a failed attempt to infringe free speech rights. And for all the lucrative opportunity that CFAs offer to solicitors and counsel, who receive money from the defendant even if the case is settled, it really should be confined by means-testing to poor plaintiffs who are reckoned by the Legal Aid Board to have a strong case. It is an irony that the new law of privacy was created by a wealthy supermodel, whose solicitors and counsel, acting on a CFA, were awarded double their usual fees for helping to create it.

One way to discourage lavish expenditures is to shine a light on them. Why should bills of costs submitted by either side not be publicised? And the costs provisions made in the confidential sections of settlement agreements ought to be public – statements in open court that damages are 'substantial' are frequently an exaggeration.

Televise the Trials

It must seem odd to viewers in Britain, watching the libel clash between Johnny Depp and Amber Heard on television direct from an American courtroom in 2022, to think that the same clash in a libel trial in London the previous year had only been accessible to them by reading newspaper accounts. Defamation trials are made for television, and neither side can sensibly object: claimants want their reputation publicly vindicated, the media argues for the public interest – why should the public be deprived of the interest in seeing the witnesses and the lawyers and deciding for themselves? The cameras could stop for any vulnerable witness, but otherwise there would be no impediment to doing justice by having it seen to be done. Even privacy cases, if the allegedly private facts had already been published, would often be appropriate for television. Courts cost a lot of money to run and some of it might be recouped by requiring television companies to pay for access.

In fact, there are a number of good reasons for allowing broadcasters, as well as court reporters, into the courts in cases which legitimately arouse public interest and which interest the public as well. Our rightly vaunted open justice principle – 'Every court in the land is open to every subject of the King' (Lord Halsbury, 1913) – serves to protect against perjury (witnesses come forward to confound lies when they hear or read of them being told), against rude or incompetent judges (publicity 'keeps the judge, while trying, under trial', said Jeremy Bentham), and it informs the public about the workings of the law. Studies in America suggest that cameras in court have this result: lawyers are better prepared, the judges are better behaved and the public is better informed. In an age when most citizens receive their news from television and the internet, and very few can actually attend court, it is absurd to confine court coverage to slim columns of print and inaccurate, almost cartoonish, drawings by 'courtroom artists'.

The ban on photographs in a British court goes back to 1925 (the last picture taken at the Old Bailey was of the infamous Dr Crippen in the dock), and all that television can offer is a sixty-second slot picturing a breathless presenter outside a court (for libel cases, on a traffic island outside the Royal Courts of Justice) with some 'artist's impressions' of the courtroom. I helped Channel 4 come up with a novel way to cater for public interest in the three-week Clive Ponting official secrets trial, by having actors read large slabs of the day's evidence for a half-hour programme at 11 p.m. each evening. I could see nothing unlawful about such a programme, but the trial judge could – he was apoplectic at the thought of an actor playing him, and overacting. We offered to replace the performers with retired newsreaders, to which he gave his approval. Of course, the director had chosen actors who would be directed to avoid imparting emotion or prejudicial mannerisms while reading the transcript: the newsreaders, excited to be back on television, over-acted. Nonetheless the programme obtained over half a million viewers each night – an indication of a genuine public interest in seeing justice done. Cameras are now allowed in appeal courts and in due course are expected to cover civil actions, and this experiment should begin with defamation trials – the coverage would certainly demonstrate the need to reform the law and its practice.

In this chapter I have described the reforms in the law that would make it more friendly to journalism that is newsworthy, in the sense of conveying information that is worth hearing and debating and questioning in a democratic society. Those reforms would end the unequal justice dispensed by defamation and privacy laws, by placing the burden of proof where it belongs, requiring claimants to negate public interest defences, abolishing the illogical 'balancing act' between Article 8 (privacy) and Article 10 (freedom of expression) so as to require all publication cases to be decided according to Article 10.

But there is another side to the defects in media law, namely the lack of any remedy for those who should be entitled to correct the record, or quickly to expunge demonstrable lies about them or to suppress truths which genuinely belong within their private spaces. For example, individuals have no right of reply to media attacks and demonisation – rights which are accorded by the laws of many European countries. In Britain, editors are exhorted by their 'codes of conduct' to afford their victims such an opportunity, if only in their letter columns, and most do, but if they do not there should be a way of requiring them to do so. Claimants who can prove serious harm caused by a publication that they can prove is fake should have a fast track to a judge empowered to make a 'declaration of falsity' and a further declaration as to how, and with what prominence, the publisher must correct it. Citizens should feel confident that the law denies the media entry to privacy zones where privacy is the expectation of everyone: the cradle, the school and the toilet, the bedroom, the hospital and the grave.

Another, and special, reason for reforming British
media laws is that they were imposed in colonial times on
no fewer than fifty-three current members of the
Commonwealth, where they are often deployed repres-
sively but with the excuse that they still exist in Britain,
ergo they cannot be contrary to freedom of expression.
The classic example was seen in Singapore, where the
prime minister Lee Kuan Yew hit upon defamation to
bankrupt his political opponents for making the mildest
of criticisms, even importing English QCs to pretend that
the massive damages, awarded by his obedient judges,
were perfectly in order. He would sue international papers
if they told inconvenient truths or reported speeches by
opposition leaders. I defended the *Far Eastern Economic
Review* over one story, and our evidence actually proved
it to be true, although it was of course held insufficient by
the judge who awarded heavy damages, which he
increased because my cross-examination 'had hurt the
Prime Minister's feelings' (whereupon the Malaysian Bar
Association put out a press release: 'This is the first
evidence that Lee Kuan Yew has any feelings'). Defamation
actions are still used by the present prime minister (Lee's
son) and other members of the ruling party, to silence
their political enemies, with the claim that they are simply
following good old English precedents.

In Hong Kong it is noticeable how newspaper editors
and protestors who cry liberty are being prosecuted and

jailed, not under the controversial national security law, but for the crime of seditious libel, negligently left behind by the British. Our laws of defamation and confidentiality are used from Mauritius and Kenya to Bermuda and Malta (where the courageous journalist Daphne Caruana Galizia was facing forty-three libel actions at the time she was assassinated). All these countries have free speech guarantees in their constitutions, but the old rules of libel cannot be struck down because they exist in the country from which they were originally derived. Thus does the myth about our 'tradition' of free speech hinder its exercise throughout what was, until recently, called the 'British' Commonwealth.

Lawfare disrupts democracy by enabling the wealthy to intimidate publishers and suppress news and opinions that the public are entitled to hear. It is, for the most part, fought below the waterline, in confidential letters between lawyers and trips to a judge in chambers behind closed doors or in the offices of taxing masters privately assessing costs. The struggles that come to the surface, like that over *Putin's People* (Roman Abramovich and the oligarchs versus Catherine Belton), only provide examples of the lawfare that has gone on exponentially since Goldsmith and Maxwell and has deterred and diminished investigative journalism, of which, as Baroness Brenda Hale points out, we need more in this country – there is so much to investigate. It is not sufficient to shame and blame the London reputation lawyers – the US Congress is now suggesting that they be denied visas and have their money confiscated if found in US banks. Nor is it enough to impose an anti-SLAPP rule on judges who will rarely apply it. Lawfare will only end when the laws are changed – they speak the only language that Messrs Sue, Grabbit and Runne understand.

Acknowledgements

I have drawn on professional experiences of advising and defending journalists and editors over the past half-century. Some have been American – from the *Wall Street Journal*, the *New York Times*, *Forbes* magazine, and of course Bill Browder – bewildered by the restrictions on free speech imposed by British law, but with the determination (and, necessarily, the funds) to fight them to the end. I am grateful, first and foremost, to my clients, and to the solicitors – notably Mark Stephens, David Hooper and Geoffrey Bindman – who entrusted me with their cases, and to Sir Andrew Nicol, for his collaboration over many editions of our textbook, *Media Law*. This book owes much to Heather Rogers KC who read it in draft, and to Iain Hunt, my editor at William Collins, and Myles Archibald, my publisher. My views have been influenced by friendships with Sir Harry Evans, Alan Rusbridger, Phil Knightly, Bruce Page, David Leigh and Tom Bower, journalists who taught me something of their trade. The inspiration to write this book came from Martin Ivens at the *Times Literary Supplement* and I must thank Sabrina Boudra for her work on the manuscript and Irena Deletic for her virtual presence.

Doughty Street Chambers
November 2022

Index